THE COMPLEAT TRAVELER'S COMPANION

COUNTRY
INNS

Lodges, and Historic
Hotels of the

West and
Southwest

by

Anthony Hitchcock

and

Jean Lindgren

BURT FRANKLIN & CO.

Published by Burt Franklin & Co.
235 East Forty-fourth Street
New York, New York, 10017

© 1979 by Burt Franklin & Co., Inc.
All rights reserved

Library of Congress Cataloging in Publication Data

Hitchcock, Anthony
Country inns, lodges, and historic hotels
of the West and Southwest

(The Compleat traveler's companion)
Includes index.
1. Hotels, taverns, etc.—The West—Directories.
2. Hotels, taverns, etc.—Southwestern States.
I. Lindgren, Jean, joint author. II. Title. III. Series.
TX907.H54   647′.9478   79-10983
ISBN 0-89102-185-X
ISBN 0-89102-160-4 (pbk.)

Designed by Bernard Schleifer

Manufactured in the United States of America

Cover illustration, courtesy of
Cobweb Palace, Westport, California

Contents

Introduction

THE WEST BECKONS US, not just the "young man" addressed by Horace Greeley, but all those who would share its treasures. And vast the treasures are. Come to the mountains, to the deserts, to the sea, and to the forests. The range of geographic and climatic conditions is as extreme in this region as anywhere on the planet. So is the range of country inns. The westward expansion is a relatively recent phenomenon, and Easterners obviously should not expect to find 200-year-old New England farmhouses. What can be found, however, is an explosion of Victorian architecture, along with dozens of hotels that hark back to the wild and woolly West. The promise of gold and silver fired the imaginations and greed of tens of thousands of prospectors and miners, who left behind dozens of ghost towns after the exhaustion of the once rich mines.

In the pages that follow, the reader will discover a wide-ranging selection of inns, lodges, and hotels. We have assembled a selection that should offer plenty of alternatives to the motel-chain syndrome that are suitable for a wide audience of readers, who will find in these pages rustic lodges, old mining camps, historic old hotels, and luxurious but interestingly eccentric resorts. We have purposely avoided a rating system, in the belief that what might rate high for us might not appeal to some of our readers. Instead, we have attempted to use description in place of an abundance of adjectives. We do not wish to have our readers unpleasantly surprised when they arrive at an inn they have chosen. Nor do we wish to impose our taste. We have remarked in other books that some places that suit our "feet in the air, relax before the fireplace" personalities might not suit readers who require more services and physical comforts than we do.

Once you have chosen an inn, we suggest that you write early for that inn's descriptive literature. Read the brochure, look at the pictures, check the map, and determine whether the inn will actually meet your needs. Inns are not like motels. Each has a special quality that can mean pleasure to one but not necessarily to another. Do not hesitate to call an innkeeper and discuss your requirements.

The quoted rates at all inns described in this book are subject to change. This is particularly true of meal prices, which reflect the highly volatile meat marketplace. Be sure to ask what the current rates are and what they include. Many inns automatically add a service charge of from 10 to 20 percent that covers all gratuities. The more expensive rooms are the ones with the best views, fireplaces, or other special features that you may or may not want. In all cases, for instance, a private bath may be expected to add from 25 to 50 percent to the basic shared-bath room rate. If your room is described as having a fireplace, be sure to ask if it can actually be used. Many insurance companies prohibit fires in guest rooms. If you have a working fireplace, ask if wood is included in the room rate. It often brings an extra charge. Although we do not detail complex rate plans, you will find that most inns offer reduced rates for stays longer than a few nights and often for off-season lodging. In some cases, inns that operate on an "all meals included" basis will rent on a lodging-only basis in the off season.

It is, of course, important to ask if your room includes meals. We have listed room rates based on the American Plan (AP, all three meals included), the Modified American Plan (MAP, breakfast and dinner included), or the European Plan (EP). Some inns use EP to indicate rooms with no meals, while others include a light continental breakfast. Our personal preference is to take rooms on the European Plan where it is offered.

Pets and small children often present special problems for the small country inn. Such inns are usually decorated with valuable antiques, and the physical arrangement of the guest and public rooms makes pets and children much more visible than they would be in a motel offering separate entrances to each guest room. A small country inn can suddenly have its mood altered by an obstreperous pet or child. For this reason many inns do not permit them to be brought. Where this is so, we have listed the fact under a special heading after that for room rates. And if pets and children are not mentioned, you should still discuss these members of your party with the innkeeper when making reservations.

The single best source of state information in a compact form is the official state road maps issued by the respective state departments of transportation. These maps can be obtained from the state department of commerce offices mentioned above or at roadside information booths within the state. Many of the maps list museums and other attractions and present concise information about the state park systems.

The inns in this book are arranged by state and, within each state, in alphabetical order according to the towns where they are situated. Readers who wish to find a particular town should consult the table of contents. An index at the end of the book lists the inns by name in alphabetical order.

The inns in this book were chosen for their inherent charm, based partially on their architectural style, location, furnishings, and history. In addition, the helpfulness of the innkeepers played a role in determining inns to be included or rejected. We used no strict definition of an "inn." Although the term usually denotes a place with both lodging and food, we have listed several that provide no meals. We did not include old inns that only serve meals, although a great many exist in the region. The information here came from several sources: our personal knowledge of the inns, recommendations of others we deem reliable, and personal surveys of innkeepers. We have made every effort to provide information as carefully and accurately as possible, but we remind readers that all rates and schedules listed are subject to change. Many inns listed as open all year may close briefly during slow periods without warning. Finally, we have neither solicited nor accepted any fees or gratuities for inclusion in this book or any of the other books in the Compleat Traveler Series.

It is very important to us that this book continue to grow in usefulness in succeeding editions. To make this possible, we depend heavily on suggestions from our readers. We very much wish to hear of your experiences at the inns listed in this volume and to receive your suggestions for additions or deletions for future volumes. We will make every effort to answer all letters personally. Please write to us in care of our publishers, Burt Franklin & Co., 235 East Forty-Fourth Street, New York, NY 10017.

Have a good trip.

JEAN LINDGREN
ANTHONY HITCHCOCK

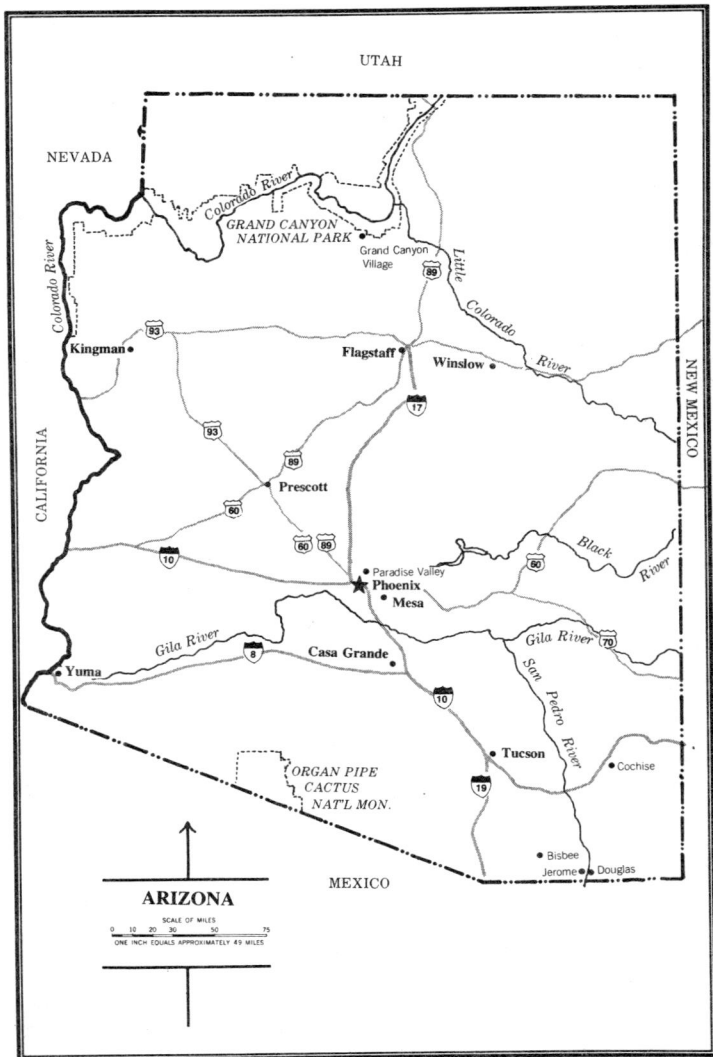

UTAH

NEVADA

NEW MEXICO

CALIFORNIA

Colorado River

GRAND CANYON
NATIONAL PARK

Grand Canyon
Village

[89]

[93]

Kingman •

Flagstaff •

Winslow •

Little Colorado River

[17]

[93]

[89]

• Prescott

[60]

[60] [89]

[10]

Black River

[80]

Paradise Valley
★ Phoenix
• Mesa

Gila River

[8]

Casa Grande •

Gila River

[70]

• Yuma

San Pedro River

[10]

ORGAN PIPE
CACTUS
NAT'L MON.

• Tucson

[19]

• Cochise

• Bisbee
Jerome • • Douglas

MEXICO

↑

ARIZONA

SCALE OF MILES
0   10   20   30   50   75
ONE INCH EQUALS APPROXIMATELY 49 MILES

Arizona

SEVERAL THOUSAND YEARS before the first Spanish exploration of this area, Indians had settled widely in Arizona. Over the centuries, the early tribes gave way to the Papago and Pima tribes, which survive today and were joined centuries ago by the Apache and the Navaho. The first Spanish explorers stumbled on the region after they had been shipwrecked near the Texas coast. The few survivors who managed to reach a small Spanish settlement near the Pacific Coast brought with them tales of incredible wealth in what they called the Seven Cities of Cibola. This led to many expeditions throughout much of the Southwest in a vain search for the treasure cities.

The first party to reach what is now Arizona was led by Marcos de Niza in 1539. He was followed almost immediately by Francisco Vasquez de Coronado. Not until the late seventeenth century, however, did any real development of the area by Europeans occur. This was a consequence of the establishment of twenty-four missions by the Roman Catholic Church. The first permanent white settlement outside the mission system was at Tubac in 1752. Tucson followed as an early fortress in 1776. When Mexico gained independence from Spain in 1822, the Arizona territory became a part of the new country. Later, after the treaties ending the Mexican War in 1848, the United States took control of New Mexico, which then included parts of Arizona.

As the conflict over slavery grew in the Eastern states, so did conflict within Arizona as to which side to espouse. In the end, the Union prevailed, and Congress established a separate Arizona Territory governed by a representative of the Union. The first governmental seat was at Fort Whipple, around which emerged the town of Prescott. For the next twenty years, the Apache tribes were a source of fear among the settlers. Numerous raiding parties were led by fierce warriors, including the famed Cochise and Geronimo. In 1886, peace with the Indian tribes was finally achieved with the surrender of Geronimo. Statehood followed in 1912.

Arizona has much appeal to tourists. A large part of it is certainly the Grand Canyon, which is visited by more tourists than practically any other natural attraction in the country. In addition, the tremendous variety of terrain—from desert to mountain—gives dimension to the state. Much of the old West lives on in towns like Tombstone and Bisbee. Even a piece of old London lives on in the form of London Bridge, recently transplanted to Lake Havusa City. The state has a particularly helpful travel promotion department, which will gladly send prospective visitors a wealth of useful travel information. Write to the State of Arizona, Office of Tourism, 1700 West Washington, Phoenix, AZ 85007. The telephone number is 602-271-3618.

Bisbee, Arizona

Bisbee, "Queen of the Mining Camps," sits on a mile-high plateau in the southeastern corner of Arizona. The county, Cochise, was named for the famous Chiricahua Apache chief who led his people in war against the United States for more than a decade in the late nineteenth century. The town of Bisbee was built with the copper fortunes made here from the most productive mines the West has ever seen. Bisbee is a history buff's and shutterbug's delight. The historic town is built on the sides of steep hills and canyon walls. It remains in appearance much the same today as it was in the raucous days of the wild West. In addition to the restored *Copper Queen Hotel*, the town has reopened the *Copper Queen Mines*, where visitors are outfitted with yellow slickers and miners' lights and led through a series of tunnels and shafts while guides explain the operations. The tour ends with a mine train ride to the outside. This tour is not for claustrophobes, but it is certainly thrilling. *The Lavender Pit* is out in the open air, where tourists can see a huge open pit mine. *Brewery Gulch* is just around the corner from the Copper Queen Hotel. The gulch was named for Muheim's Brewery and at one time boasted forty bars and a great number of ladies of the evening.

COPPER QUEEN HOTEL

11 Howell Street, Bisbee, AZ. Mailing address: P.O. Box Drawer C.Q., Bisbee, AZ 85603. 602-432-2216. *Innkeepers*: Richard and Virginia Hort. Open all year.

The Copper Queen Hotel, once considered the finest hotel in the West, is named for the most productive and famous underground copper mine in the West. Since the gigantic copper finds of the 1870s the town has been known as the "Queen of the Mining Camps." Shortly after the turn of the century, the huge, wealthy Copper Mining Camp (later merged to become the Phelps Dodge Corporation) built the elegant Copper Queen Hotel to house the many mining executives, traveling salesmen in the copper business, territorial governors, and flamboyant characters attracted to this boom town.

The Copper Queen Properties purchased the old hotel and have restored it to the grandeur of its heyday. This restoration is an ongoing project, with very successful results so far. The hotel is, refreshingly, being resurrected as the elegant lady of the early to mid-1900s. The original furnishings have received face-lifts; the hotel actually looks not like a restoration, but rather as if it had never changed. Guests enter the ground-floor lobby and sign in at the old front dest with its creaky old cash register and original switchboard. The sturdy old Victor Safe is guarded by the handsome wall clock above it, its pendulum still marking time as it has since the hotel's beginnings. The furnishings of this room and the second floor guest lounge are pure "1920s–1930s hotel." The massive pieces of furniture are leather-cushioned and ornately carved wood.

The rooms throughout are furnished with antiques and "near antiques" of the 1920s through the 1940s. The forty-six guest rooms vary from spacious, high-ceiling affairs to cozy, intimate little nests. All of the rooms have private baths or showers; some have the old clawfooted tubs, The previous owner, in a burst of enthusiasm for the color red, papered the upper floors with flocked red bordello-style wallpaper and laid down a great deal of shaggy red carpeting.

The Copper Queen Saloon and Dining Room are off either side of the lobby. The saloon has a nostalgic bar and many cartoon sketches of local town characters past and present, and plenty of celebrities who have appeared here while on location for the many films shot in town. The dining room has crisp blue and white gingham checkered tablecloths, period décor, and tall windows looking out to the mountains across the street. The menu features hearty Western-style meals of steaks, ribs, and poultry. A big favorite is duckling. The dessert specialty is a delicious homemade carrot cake. The hotel serves three meals a day to guests and public alike. Both the saloon and the dining room offer liquor and a selection of wines. *Room Rates*: Singles range from $12 to $28 and doubles from $14 to $32, depending on location and size of room (EP). *Pets*: Not allowed. *Driving Instructions*: The town is 90 miles southeast of Tucson. Take I-10 east to Route 80 and then Route 80 to Bisbee.

Cochise, Arizona

Cochise is a small town in the heart of the former Apache stronghold about 85 miles east of Tucson and 65 miles north of the Mexican border. As you drive through the area, the exploits of the Western heroes of the dime novels of yesterday seem to live again behind every rock and over every bluff. About 15 miles to the northeast is the town of Wilcox, site of the *Cochise Visitor Center*. The museum contains important exhibits relating to the Apache Indian heritage and the history and culture of Cochise County. From Cochise one can take a one- or two-day circular tour of Cochise County that includes the old copper-mining town of Bisbee; Tombstone, the town that wouldn't die; and the border village of Douglas.

THE COCHISE HOTEL

Cochise Road, Cochise, AZ. Mailing address: Box 27, Cochise,
AZ 85606. 602-384-3156. *Innkeeper*: Lillie Harrington. Open all
year by reservation only.

If you happen to have a Wells Fargo stagecoach at your disposal, you
will in no way feel out of place arriving at the Cochise. Built in 1882
of thick adobe, the hotel stands at the former junction of the Southern
Pacific and old Arizona Eastern railways. The long front hallway
contained the Wells Fargo office that handled the ore shipments
from the Johnson and Pearce mines of an era gone by. The office still
exists, and the old Greene Cattle Company safe still stands in its
original spot.

Cross the threshold of the Cochise today and you are transported
instantly back to turn-of-the-century Arizona. The furnishings are
authentic pieces from the nineteenth century: a wind-up phono-
graph, heavy walnut tables and chairs, rocking chairs, a carved wooden
sofa upholstered in tan velvet (reputed to have belonged to Jenny
Lind), a huge wardrobe with mirrored doors, and other pieces of the
period all arranged with formality around an Oriental carpet. A painted
china and brass chandelier with dropping crystal pendants and period
table lamps add their soft glow.

The five guest rooms carry out the period theme with furnishings
that provide comfort while at the same time preserving the earlier
era. Each guest room has had a modern bathroom and heating installed, but the improvements are in no way intrusive. The menu in

the dining room is a simple one. With the exception of breakfast, all meals offer a choice of broiled steak or chicken. The meals are served family style, with vegetables, salad, potatoes, and hot rolls. All meals are by reservation only. *Room Rates*: Singles are $10.50, doubles $12.50, and suites $18.50. *Pets*: Permitted by special arrangement only. *Driving Instructions*: Take I-10 to Route 666, then drive south 5 miles to Cochise Road.

Douglas, Arizona

Douglas is a border town of 12,000 located in the extreme southeastern corner of the state. The town is a good stopover for people who wish to explore the *Coronado National Forest* and *Chiricahua National Monument* to the northeast and Tombstone and the *Cochise Stronghold Recreation Area* to the northwest. The Stronghold was the hiding place of the great Apache chief for many years in the late nineteenth century. Douglas offers easy access to the Mexican city of Acua Prieta, just across the border in Sonora. One day's travel to the border cities such as Acua Prieta is an easy matter. No special permits are required for U.S. citizens, providing they go no more than 15 miles into Mexico. Most Mexican stores will gladly accept U.S. currency, so money need not be exchanged. Visitors traveling in and out of Mexico are advised to leave luggage at their U.S. hotel or inn because the presence of luggage will be likely to cause serious delays for customs checks. For extended trips beyond the border, consult your nearest Mexican tourist agency or Mexican Consulate for detailed travel information. The U.S. Customs Office, Washington, D.C. 20226, also has useful travel information about passing through customs with minimal delay. Its free pamphlets outline what may be brought across the border legally and without customs duty.

GADSDEN HOTEL
   1046 G Avenue West, Douglas, AZ 85607. 602-364-2411. *Innkeeper*: Vernon I. Carnes. Open all year.
The Gadsden is a classic Southwestern hotel built under the inspired direction of an Italian architect in 1927 to replace an old wood-frame hotel that had stood on the same site. The present five-story building bears distinctive elaborate formed-concrete ornamentation encrust-

ing its exterior, but it is in the lobby that the scope and magnitude of the Italianate design are most apparent. In the middle of the lobby is a wide set of marble stairs, which mount to the fifth floor. At the mezzanine level, a huge stained-glass depiction of a desert scene sparkles in the daylight, as bright today as it was in 1930, when it was installed by Tiffany's of New York. From the center of the lobby rise immense polished marble columns decorated at their tops with solid gold leaf. Gold leaf continues across the entire ceiling, broken only by two stained-glass sunlights, also by Tiffany's.

The hotel was named for James Gadsden, who engineered the Gadsden Purchase of all of Cochise County from Mexico in 1853. The Mexican bandit and folk hero Pancho Villa fought many skirmishes with the Texas Rangers near Douglas. During his final battle, only 5 miles from the previous Gadsden Hotel, guests gathered on the roof to watch the fighting. In the heat of the battle between Villa and the Rangers from El Paso, the bullets began to ricochet off the hotel's elevator housing and the guests were forced to retreat hastily to the safety of the lobby below. In view of the architectural significance of the building, and the historical interest of the site, former Governor Castro declared the Gadsden to be a state historical monument a few years ago.

The public rooms of the hotel include the lobby, a dress shop, a beauty shop, the DeGrazia Art Gallery, the Castilian Dining Room, a modern coffee shop and grill, and the Saddle and Spur Lounge, whose walls bear the brands of more than two thousand ranches from all over the world. The backbar is the original, fashioned from cherry wood, but the rest of the room was modernized over the years. The dining room is done in a classic Spanish motif, with ornate carved wood and the original Spanish murals. It serves Spanish-American food at very low prices. The restaurant has à la carte and complete-dinner service featuring a salad bar, relishes, and homemade soups and entrées. A house specialty is a Mexican influenced soup consisting of chili-flavored meatballs in a spicy broth with rice. The kitchen prepares several steak dishes including a Spanish cube steak baked with tomatoes, onions, and spices. Also on the menu frequently are chicken cacciatora, Swiss steak, prime ribs, and tenderloin tips with noodles. Prices for complete meals are in the $6 to $7 range.

The 147 guest rooms and four suites are on the four floors above the lobby. Two floors have been fully modernized and have reproduction heavy Spanish furnishings and Spanish décor. The other two retain the style and furnishings of the 1920s with heavy wooden furniture. Rooms typically have one or more beds, a chest, easy chairs, color television, and air conditioning. The bathrooms have the original handmade Mexican tiles and fully modern fixtures.

This hotel is popular with tour groups and individuals who appreciate its nearness to the Mexican border (just five minutes away) and its architectural splendor. The lobby is frequently the scene of a fashion show or private party. There are several banquet and meeting rooms, consistent with its being a large, full-service hotel. *Room Rates*: Singles are $19, doubles are $21, and suites are $25 to $45. Children under twelve are free. *Driving Instructions*: The hotel, in downtown Douglas, can be reached via either Route 80 or Route 666.

Grand Canyon Village, Arizona

Grand Canyon Village is the major tourist focus for visits to the south rim of *Grand Canyon National Park*. Ask almost any group of Americans which sight they would rather see than any other and the resounding winner would be Grand Canyon. Its miles of vistas enchant visitors from sunrise to sunset and from season to season. Accessible all year, the south rim is the most popular starting point for visits to the most magnificent canyon in the world. Short drives from Grand Canyon Village will bring visitors to vantage points where the walls of the canyon can be seen shifting from color to color as the sun changes position throughout the day. Upon arriving at the park, it is best to check in at the *Visitor Center* at the east end of Grand Canyon Village. Here, maps and pamphlets are available to help visitors plan trips along the rim in both directions. There are two museums maintained by the park service at the south rim. *Tusayan Museum*, about a half hour's drive east from Grand Canyon Village, is located at the site of a Pueblo ruin that is about eight hundred years old. Many visitors to the canyon take float trips down the Colorado River—an excellent way to see the canyon from inside. These take several days and are booked through approximately twenty outfitters currently licensed by the park to provide this service. Ask the park office or the registration desk at Bright Angels Lodge for further information. Guides are also available for conducted hiking tours. Visitors to the canyon are urged to remember that the hike to the canyon floor involves a descent of almost a vertical mile over trails that are 7 to 10 miles long, and that the climb back to the top is strenuous. Those who are not in excellent health should enjoy the splendors of the park from above, where the many lookout points and park services provide ample opportunities to enjoy many of the park's more than 1 million acres. For further information about Grand Canyon National Park, consult the Park Supervisor, Grand Canyon National Park, Grand Canyon, AZ 86023; the telephone number is 602-638-2411. Still more information can be obtained from the two park hotel concessionaires listed in the following lodge writeup.

PHANTOM RANCH

Grand Canyon, AZ 86023. 602-638-2302. *Innkeeper*: Don Weir. Open all year.

Phantom Ranch is far and away the most remote of the lodges we discuss. The lodge lies at the bottom of the Grand Canyon and is accessible only by foot or on muleback. To reach the lodge, one takes trails that depart from either the north or south rim. The north-rim trails are open only May through October, but the south rim remains active all year. Reservations are absolutely essential at the lodge and can be made directly or by inquiring at the transportation desk of Bright Angel Lodge at the south rim. Although it is possible to make reservations for two-day mule pack trips to the lodge and back from the south rim, travelers are advised that there is often a three- to six-month waiting period for mule reservations. The hike to the lodge from the south rim is over either of two trails, one of 7.3 miles and one of 9.8 miles. Both trails involve crossing one of two suspension bridges, and both are modestly strenuous. The longer trail has a camping area partway down, so the trip may be divided into two stages if desired. Even though no charge is levied at the campground, reservations are mandatory there as well.

When you arrive at the Phantom Ranch, you are greeted by a long stone lodge and fifteen cabins. The lodge has a rough stucco interior and has been divided into a dining hall, kitchen, employees' dining hall, and storage areas. The stone for the lodge and the cabins was gathered locally when construction began in the 1920s. The lodge furniture consists mostly of strung rawhide chairs, and the feeling throughout is rustic Southwestern.

Each cabin is heated and contains four single beds, a desk, and two chairs. Coolers are also provided, as well as a sink with running cold water and a toilet, but there are no showers in the cabins, the only hot water and showers for guests being in the shower house.

The ranch serves two meals per day, and sandwiches are available for lunch at the snack bar. Both meals are served to a maximum of forty-four people, with guests being given preference for meals and then any extra meals being available to those camping on the nearby canyon-floor campground. Breakfast consists of eggs, bacon, juice, bread, and coffee served family style. The charge for breakfast is $4.04. Dinner, priced at $9.57 and likewise a family-style affair, consists of steak, mashed potatoes, gravy, vegetables, bread, cake, and a beverage.

Those who prefer to see the canyon from above, avoiding the strenuous trip to the floor as well as the relatively Spartan accommodations, are urged to consult the Grand Canyon National Park Lodges, Grand Canyon, AZ 86023 (phone: 602-638-2631). They have more than six hundred rooms and suites and more than a hundred cabins on the south rim. Their full-service facilities are open all year. TWA Services, Inc., has a lodge with 180 units at the north rim, but it is open in the summer only. For further information write those people at Box 400, Cedar City, Utah 84720 or telephone them at 801-586-9476. *Room Rates*: Rooms at Phantom Ranch are $27 for two, with an additional $7 for each additional person. Dorm facilities are available at $8.24 per person and are segregated for men and women. *Pets*: Not permitted by the Park Authority. *Driving Instructions*: Take Route 64 north from I-40 to the park village of Grand Canyon. Report to Bright Angel Lodge to confirm reservations at Phantom Ranch and get instructions on the alternative trails to the canyon floor. Those hiking to the bottom from the north rim (summers only and with advance reservations required) must get instructions in advance from Phantom Ranch.

Jerome, Arizona

In the old mining days, Jerome was a wild and woolly place filled with miners drawn to the area by the tremendous copper mines operating in the area. In its heyday, Jerome boasted a population of 15,000. Millions of dollars' worth of copper were taken from mines such as the "Little Daisy" and the huge Phelps Dodge United Verde Mine. Visitors should not miss the *Jerome Historic State Park* or the *Historical Society Mine Museum*. The latter is located in the old Douglas mansion, once occupied by the Douglas family, who owned some of the largest mines in the area. The town of Douglas was later named for Mr. Douglas. The museum houses many items of mining memorabilia and is a good starting place for exploring the region. Jerome is adjacent to Cleopatra Mountain, which rises to about 5,000 feet. The views of the Verde Valley, the red-rock country of Sedona, and the San Francisco Peaks in the distance, as well as the remains of the mining camps and old town stores, make the village a scenic stop for travelers in the central part of the state.

CONNOR HOTEL

Box 12, Jerome, AZ 86331. 602-634-5792. *Innkeeper*: Terry Watt. Open all year.

Terry Watt has fixed up seven rooms in the old Connor Hotel, which has stood where it is now for the past eighty years. The first floor of this two-story brick-front hotel is devoted to a curio shop, an antique shop, a gallery, and a bar. Upstairs, there used to be many small rooms, but Terry combined several pairs of rooms to create a total of seven rooms, five of which have private baths. The flavor of the place is decidedly old fashioned, with sparse furnishings and period ceiling lighting. The rooms are all carpeted. Probably the nicest in the hotel is the Skylight Room, which has brass beds and a private bath. The hotel serves no meals, but three restaurants are nearby. *Room Rates*: Ask the management for the latest rates, which were unavailable when this book went to press. *Pets*: Not permitted. *Driving Instructions*: Jerome is located about 40 miles northeast of Prescott and 60 miles southwest of Flagstaff on Route 89A.

Paradise Valley, Arizona

Paradise Valley is, along with Scottsdale, a part of the northeastern suburban core of Phoenix. As with all urban areas represented in this book, space does not permit a thorough discussion of the area attractions. A representative selection follows. The *Phoenix Art Museum* is a fine, wide-ranging museum with collections representing North America, Europe, and the Orient. It is at 1625 North Central Avenue and is open daily except Mondays; there is no charge for admission. The *Heard Museum of Anthropology and Primitive Arts* is a major center for Indian displays and arts and crafts exhibits. The museum is at 22 East Monte Vista Road; it is open daily with nominal admission charges. The *Phoenix Zoo* at 60th Street and East Van Buren has a worldwide collection of animals. It is open daily and an admission is charged. The *Desert Botanical Garden* in Papago Park, with access from 58th Street and Van Buren or 64th Street and McDowell, contains more than a thousand different cacti and other unusual plants in a natural setting. For further area information contact the Phoenix and Valley of the Sun Convention and Visitors Bureau, 2701 East Camelback Road, Phoenix AZ 85061. The telephone number is 602-957-0070.

HERMOSA INN

5532 North Palo Cristi Road, Paradise Valley, AZ 85253. 602-955-8660. *Innkeepers*: Eckard (Ike) and Angy Bauer. Open all year except July and August.

The Hermosa Inn is a Southwestern hacienda with an interesting history that dates back almost fifty years. In 1930, cowboy-artist Lon Megargee completed his Casa Hermosa (handsome house), a rambling Spanish-Colonial hacienda. The structure, typical of Megargee's style of life and painting, was constructed without formal blueprints and guided only by inspiration. Scion of an old Philadelphia family, exhibition roper, rancher, town fireman, and poker dealer, Megargee was a self-taught artist who gained considerable fame. He did a series of paintings for the Arizona Capitol and later became famous for two paintings commissioned by an Arizona brewery, *Black Bart* and *Cowboy's Dream*. As Megargee's hacienda gradually expanded through the addition of other buildings, Megargee decided to convert his residence into a guest ranch. A few years later he sold out and moved on.

What he left behind was a beautiful main lodge and individual guest cottages. Many of the original structural features including secret passages, beehive fireplaces, massive doors, and handsome iron work remain today. From its tiled roof to the adobe turrets to its heavy beams and wooden ceilings, the effect is something like a Mexican-Spanish-rustic blend. Accommodations are thoroughly modern within the rustic décor. Every room has combination tub and shower, color television, telephone, and a private patio. Guest facilities range from rooms with queen-sized or two double beds, to efficiencies in the casitas, to villa suites with living room, kitchen, two bedrooms and two bathrooms. On the grounds are five tennis courts (with a tennis pro), a heated pool, and shuffleboard.

The à la carte dinner menu has choices of eleven entrées including prime ribs, filet mignon, shishkebab, fillet of sole amandine, rainbow trout, king crab legs, scampi, chicken, and veal picatta. Prices range from $7.95 to $8.95, with additional charges for starters and desserts. The luncheon menu lists several hot and cold sandwiches, grilled items, and salad plates. All luncheons are under $5. *Room Rates*: Rooms range from $20 to $80 in the summer to $40 to $150 in the high season from mid-January to mid-April. All rooms are EP. *Pets*: Not permitted. *Driving Instructions*: The inn is on Palo Cristi Road (also called 36th Street), south of its intersection with Lincoln Drive in Paradise Valley.

Tucson, Arizona

Tucson lies in a bowl-like depression surrounded by a ring of mountains and miles of desert. With an hour's drive one can leave the sweltering heat of the center of the city and be high in the mountains among the pines and snow in the winter. Tucson is in the land of the Saguaro, the stately cactus that perhaps best represents the outsider's notion of what a true desert should be. Among the area's diverse sights are the *San Xavier Mission*, which dates from the late eighteenth century; the *Arizona-Sonora Desert Museum*, where the visitor can see otters play in special glass-walled tanks and numerous displays on desert life; and *Old Tucson*, a western movie location *par excellence*. Within the city limits, the *Arizona Historical Society* at Second Street and Park Avenue and the *Tucson Museum of Art* at 235 West Alameda are logical stopping places for first-time visitors. For further area information, write the Tucson Convention and Visitors Bureau, Box 27210, Tucson AZ 85726, or call 602-791-4768.

HACIENDA DEL SOL

Hacienda Del Sol Road, Tucson, AZ 85718. 602-299-1501. *Innkeeper*: Robert Hartman. Open from November 1 to May 1.

Hacienda Del Sol is one of the truly elegant ranch-inns in the Southwest. The inn was originally constructed as a nondenominational preparatory school for girls using the architectural design of Josias T. Joesler. The exclusive boarding school finally closed its doors when it could not assemble a topnotch faculty under the pressures of World War II. It reopened as a resort inn in 1945 and passed through several hands until the Hartmans purchased it in 1970.

The Hartmans set about to renovate the fine old adobe structure in high-style Mexican form with stucco arches, heavy, dark exposed beams, and a fine collection of decorative Mexican and Indian art, accessories, and handcrafts. In addition to the original buildings, the Hartmans have built several carefully designed cottage-casitas, a tennis court, an enclosed therapy pool, and an exercise room. Each of the public rooms has broad expanses of stuccoed walls broken by broad expanses of glass offering vistas of the surrounding desert or the Catalina Mountains. Doorways are often accented with hand-painted tile, and the doors themselves bear the Spanish look of heavy panels. Each of the forty-five guest rooms has its own private bath.

Although it is on the outskirts of Tucson, the Hacienda del Sol has become one of its more famous eating spots, mostly because of its Cordon Bleu chef, Arne Hoelli of Norway. Hoelli and his most capable collection of underchefs put out two daily *prix fixe* meals plus a standard breakfast, available to the public as well as guests.

The evening meal ($10) starts with one of Chef Hoelli's large repertoire of soups. His own favorites include an unusual French carrot or the popular Garbure soup. The dinner includes a choice of two or three entrées such as chicken Norwegian (browned, then roasted, and finally fried crisp and decorated with french fried parsley), fried trout in sour cream sauce, poached salmon Hollandaise, or prime ribs with Yorkshire pudding. This is followed by a choice of several fine pies and cakes created by the inn's seventy-year-old pastry chef (he's been cooking professionally since he was twelve). On Tuesday evenings, the inn offers its famous adobe oven dinner.

The Hacienda Del Sol is a very special place. Its rates are reasonable in view of the fact that meals are included. Because the inn is also a ranch, horseback riding is available. *Room Rates*: Rooms range from $45 to $65 per day, single rooms AP (all meals) and from $85 to $95 per day, double occupancy, AP. All resort facilities, including health pool, regular pool, tennis, and health center, are included. *Driving Instructions*: Take I-10 to River Road, then River Road to Hacienda Del Sol Road.

THE LODGE ON THE DESERT

306 North Alvernon Way, Tucson, AZ. Mailing address: Box 42500, Tucson, AZ 85733. 602-325-3366. *Innkeeper*: Schuyler W. Lininger. Open all year.

The Lodge on the Desert is styled after a Mexican hacienda, and the décor throughout is completely under the Mexican-Spanish influence. The lodge was started by the parents of the present innkeeper and was his family home for many years. Over the years, it has gradually expanded from its original nine rooms to its present thirty-five guest rooms plus a number of public rooms.

The orientation at the lodge is toward outdoor living. Even inside, one has a lovely view of the Santa Catalina mountains to the north. The feeling of old Mexico and the flavor of the Southwest are captured within the patio walls of the lodge. There are adobe-colored *casas* with their *ocotillo* covered porches, intimate Spanish courtyards, spacious lawns, and flower-filled gardens. Inside, the heavy original beams and broad expanses of plastered walls, exposed wooden lintels over the windows, and tin chandeliers enhance the hacienda feeling. The guestrooms, like the public rooms, have a Spanish look with beamed ceilings and warm wooden floors. More than half of the guest rooms have their own wood-burning fireplaces, and all have their own tiled bathrooms.

The lodge takes special pride in its food service. Breakfasts are served in each guest room from a menu with several choices. Each breakfast is cooked to order and then delivered to the room at no additional charge. Lunch and dinner are served in the Mexican tiled dining rooms of which one is noted for its impressive fluted Mexican fireplace. During the period of the year when the American Plan is in effect (the cooler months), the dining room offers a limited menu with four entrées at lunch and four at dinner. A typical selection of lunch choices might include french friend turkey with almond sauce, broccoli supreme, beef tostado, and baked ham loaf with mustard sauce. Quiche is a frequent luncheon choice. Luncheon entrées are priced at $2.75 with appetizers and desert extra. Dinners are always preceeded by a homemade soup such as spinach and oyster soup, Chantilly soup, or the Lodge at the Desert special "glorified" chicken soup. Entrée choices usually include a daily roast such as lamb, loin of pork, or beef, as well as choices like chicken Maryland with horse-radish sauce, fillet of sole *bonne-femme*, or veal parmesan with fetucini. *Room Rates*: In general the lodge operates on the American Plan during the cooler months and on the European Plan at all times. American Plan rates for double rooms are $68 to $100 per couple, per day, depending on the elegance of the room chosen. European Plan rates are $46 to $78 in the cooler months and $30 to $56 per couple, per day in the summer. Single rates are available. *Driving Instructions*: The inn is in the center of Tucson near the University of Arizona campus. Take Broadway from I-10 to North Alvernon and the lodge.

California

CALIFORNIA WAS FIRST explored by the Spaniard Juan Rodriguez Cabrillo in 1542. He and his crew were on a mission to explore the Pacific Coast. Although he died while the mission was only partly completed, his crew continued up the coast as far as what is now Oregon. In 1579, Sir Francis Drake claimed California for the English, based on his explorations in that year. Both England and Spain vied for early control of California as they established strongholds in different parts of the region. Although Spain had established a strong mission system in the region known as Lower California or the Baja (now part of Mexico), there were no missions in the rest of California until 1769, when the mission at San Diego was established. By 1823, the number of Spanish missions had reached twenty-one. During this period, Russian explorers were creating settlements along the coast north of what is today San Francisco. These settlers, considered a threat by the Spanish, held their settlements and, in some cases, built fortifications until the 1840s, when Russia signed treaties withdrawing the settlements.

California came under Mexican rule after Mexico gained its independence in 1822. In the ensuing years, the Mexican hold on the territory dwindled as American settlers came to the region in growing numbers. Among the early American settlers were men like Kit Carson and Jedediah Smith. California became a part of the United States after the end of the Mexican War in 1848. That same year saw the discovery of gold near John Sutter's sawmill on the American River. California would never be the same as hordes of miners descended on the territory, swelling its population from 20,000 to more than 400,000 in just twelve years. Statehood was granted in 1850, and today California is one of the largest states in area and the leader

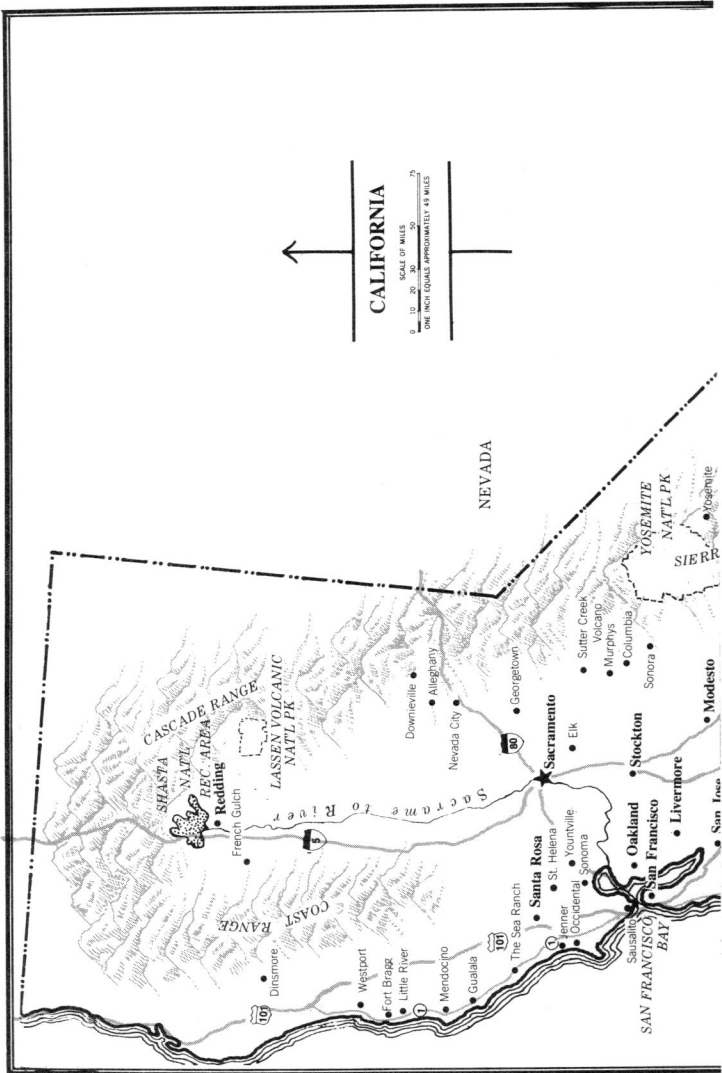

CALIFORNIA

SCALE OF MILES

0   10   20   30   50   75

ONE INCH EQUALS APPROXIMATELY 49 MILES

NEVADA

YOSEMITE
NAT'L PK

SIERR

CASCADE RANGE

SHASTA
NAT'L
REC. AREA
Redding

LASSEN VOLCANIC
NAT'L PK

French Gulch

Sacramento River

COAST RANGE

Downieville

Allegheny

Nevada City

Georgetown

Sutter Creek
Volcano
Murphys
Columbia
Sonora

Sacramento

Elk

Stockton

Modesto

Oakland

Livermore

San Jose

Santa Rosa

St. Helena
Yountville

Sonoma

Occidental

The Sea Ranch

Jenner

Sausalito

San Francisco

SAN FRANCISCO BAY

Dinsmore

Westport

Fort Bragg

Little River

Mendocino

Gualala

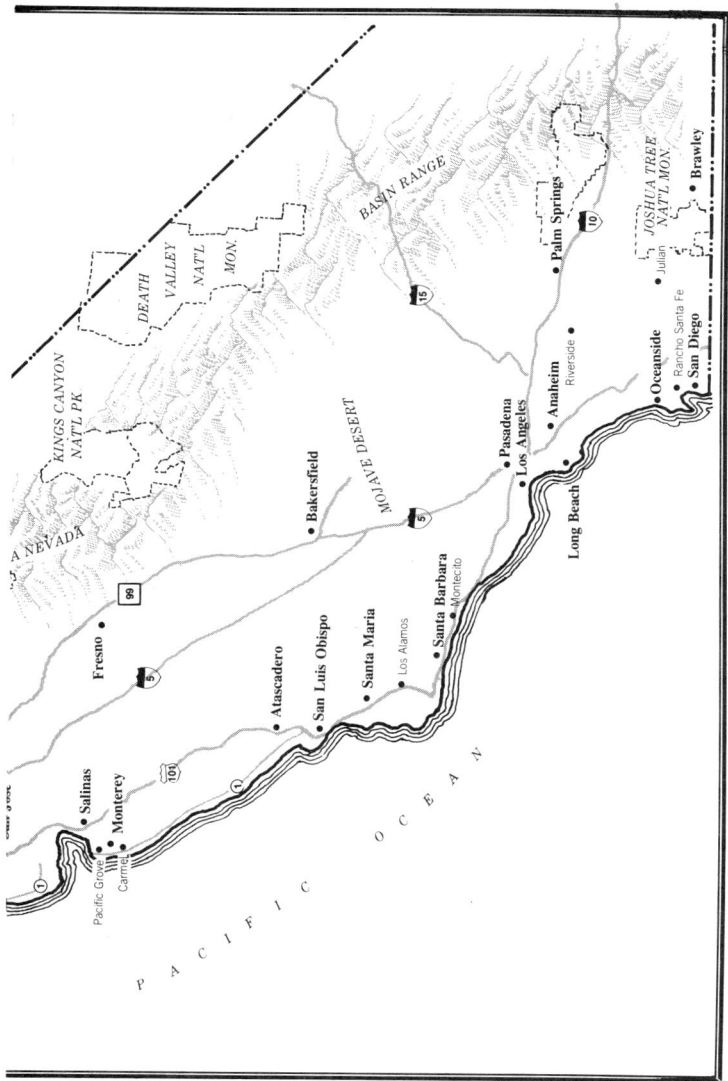

in population. It is more than 700 miles long and as wide as 360 miles at its widest point. Its terrain includes towering mountains, broad desert land, and vast agricultural flatlands that produce much of the country's vegetable crop and wine from its vineyards. California has only recently instituted a statewide travel promotion department, and much of this work is still being handled at the local level through chambers of commerce. However, some material is available from Office of Visitor Services, Department of Economic and Business Development, 1120 N Street, P.O. Box 1499, Sacramento, CA 95805. The telephone number is 916-322-1396.

Alleghany, California

Alleghany is an off-the-beaten-track former mining village in the heart of the Gold Country, about 80 miles northeast of Sacramento. The village was founded in the 1850s by a group of Hawaiian sailors who had jumped ship in San Francisco and were lured by the promise of gold into the hill country. The mountainous hamlet saw the close of the last gold mine, the famous Sixteen-to-One mine, in 1965. It was one of the longest-operating mines in the state and one of only a handful that continued to mine after World War II. Today, the mining town is a quiet and restful place that offers plenty of hiking, fishing, and relaxing on the piney slopes. Gold panning is still a popular activity, and the innkeepers at the lodge that follows will be happy to rent gold pans as well as give tours of the old Kenton Mine.

KENTON MINE LODGE
Foote Crossing Road, Alleghany, CA. Mailing address: Box 942, Alleghany, CA 95910. 916-287-3212. *Innkeepers*: Joan and Al Weiss. Open from May 1 to November 1.
Here is one of the most peaceful settings a vacationer could find anywhere. The Kenton Mine Lodge is a rustic old mining camp that housed miners from the historic gold mines of the Sierras. It last housed miners from the Oriental Mine.

Al and Joan Weiss, both antique collectors and restorers, bought the old mining camp and completely restored it. The buildings have been redone, and whatever furnishings were lacking have been replaced with period antiques that bring to mind the colorful days of the Forty-niners. The old beds are covered with patchwork quilts, and the rooms contain some of the furniture and decorations fashioned by the miners themselves. There are seven cabins along the creek amid towering pine trees. Each cabin has two bedrooms and a bath. The boarding house, used by the unmarried miners, contains nine guest rooms and five baths. The entire camp sits in a canyon at an elevation of 3,500 feet in the foothills of the High Sierras. The nights can get quite cool, so be sure to bring warm sweaters and, in general, casual clothing.

The Weisses serve hearty home-cooked meals in the family style around big tables in the Cook House. Wine and beer accompany the meals. In the warm, informal atmosphere, guests have a chance to meet and get to know one another. The Mine Tavern is a central meeting area where guests can join in folksinging, chatting, and, occasionally, informal seminars. Joan and Al also show films and invite guest speakers here for interested guests and friends. During the day, the peaceful, relaxing enjoyment to be found in the surrounding foothills and little mountain streams includes exploring, hiking, fishing, and just sitting and taking in the fresh mountain air. *Room Rates*: Cabins are $30.00 per person, double occupancy. Additional adults are $26.50, and children less, AP. The Boarding House rooms are $27.50 per person. Rooms and cabins are less by the week. *Driving Instructions*: Take Route 49 north of Nevada City through Grass Valley, watching for the left turn marked Downieville. About five miles past the town of North San Juan, take the turn to the right to the town of Alleghany. From Alleghany, take Foote's Crossing Road, the first road to the right after entering town, for 2½ miles. Take the left-hand fork to the lodge.

Carmel California

Carmel has been a popular retreat for artists, authors, professors, and the wealthy from the San Francisco Bay area since the turn of the century. As a consequence, it has become a popular tourist town that blends the quaint and the chic in its shops and its architecture. The artist colony survives, although somewhat elbowed aside by the crowds of the summer months. There are dozens of galleries, antique shops, and unusual stores, and outstanding restaurants. Carmel has a lovely white sand beach although its cold, sometimes treacherous waters often preclude swimming here. The *Mission San Carlos Borromeo del Rio Carmelo* is beautifully restored. The mission is open almost every day except some holidays. *Point Lobos Game Reserve* is located to the south of the village on Route 1. It is home for many varieties of water birds, including the nearly extinct brown pelican, seals, and the playful sea otter. Between November and February, whales can often be seen on their southward migration.

The *Seventeen Mile Drive*, between Carmel and Monterey, is particularly scenic as it meanders through the Del Monte Forest past spectacular ocean scenes and luxurious homes. A $3 toll is charged for the trip. The *Carmel Bach Festival* is held in late July, and the *Carmel Mission Fiesta* is the fourth Sunday in September. Nearby Monterey is a most important tourist stop with numerous museums chronicling a history that stretches from the earliest Spanish mission days through the westward expansion. At least a full day is needed to enjoy even a significant fraction of the sights.

THE CYPRESS INN

Seventh and Lincoln, Carmel, CA. Mailing address: Box Y, Carmel, CA 93921. 408-624-3871. *Innkeeper*: Max McKee. Open all year.

The Cypress Inn is a moderately large inn with 33 guest rooms fashioned in the Mediterranean-style architecture so popular in southern California and the Southwest. The long, cathedral-ceilinged lobby has high beams, polished tile, stucco walls, chandeliers, and a deep-red and gold patterned rug. At the end of the lobby is a huge fireplace, and draped French windows open onto a flower-bedecked courtyard. The lobby is decorated with a collection of antiques from the nineteenth century, and the walls are hung with paintings of the pre-Picasso period. The courtyard is of red brick, and its furniture is white wrought iron.

Guest rooms at the Cypress range from singles to king-size suites, all of which have color television and private bath. They have shuttered windows, burnt-orange rugs, and furniture of recent vintage that has been antiqued. Probably the favorite guest room is the one in the tower, which affords a 270-degree panoramic view of the village. *Room Rates*: The rates are from $24 to $48, double occupancy. All room rates include a continental breakfast, the only meal served.

Pets: Not permitted. *Driving Instructions*: The inn is off Route 1 in the heart of Carmel.

HOLIDAY HOUSE

Camino Real, Carmel, CA. Mailing address: P.O. Box 234, Carmel, CA 93921. *Innkeepers*: Kenneth and Janet Weston. Open all year.

Holiday House was built in 1905 as a summer cottage by a Stanford University botany professor. It was converted to an inn in the 1920s and has been taking in guests ever since under a series of owners and managers. Its early conversion to innkeeping makes the Holiday House the oldest guest house in Carmel. It is a shingled cottage with dormers and porches poking out in all directions.

The atmosphere here is casual and restful. Guests relax in the living room, on the sunporch, and, in nice weather, on the sunny terrace overlooking the extensive garden. The living room has a rough stone fireplace in which a fire burns on cool mornings and evenings. Books and games are available to guests, and so is a grand piano. Guest rooms (there are six, of which two have private baths) are furnished in turn-of-the-century décor with many antiques, some original art work reflecting the artist colony present in Carmel, and fresh flowers. Rooms that share a bath have washbasins. We particularly like the guest rooms with sloping ceilings, which add a cozy feeling. Several guest rooms and the living room share a pleasant view of the ocean.

This inn is only three blocks from the beach and the same distance from the center of town. Thus one can shed the family car on arrival

and explore the village on foot, having to contend only with the frequent crowding of other eager tourists. Don't be surprised if some of your fellow guests can recall their visits here more than thirty years ago. One woman came for years as a child accompanied by her grandmother, then returned as an adult recently to be pleasantly surprised that "her old Holiday House" was still the same.

Janet serves a continental breakfast-plus each morning; it includes hot roll, coffee cake or muffin, choice of cereal, juice, and choice of coffee, tea, or hot chocolate. Often she will include a plate of cheeses and fresh fruit. *Room Rates*: Rooms with private bath are $23 for a single and $25 for a double. Shared-bath rates are $2 less. *Pets*: Not permitted. *Driving Instructions*: From Highway 1 take Ocean Avenue exit in Carmel, continue through town to Camino Real, and turn south one block to the inn.

THE PINE INN

Ocean Avenue at Monte Verde Street, Carmel-by-the-Sea, CA. Mailing address: Box 250, Carmel-by-the-Sea, CA 93921. 408-624-3851. *Innkeeper*: Max McKee. Open all year.

Pine Inn is a moderately large, posh Victorian inn with varied and elegant furnishings and full services concomitant with a small first-class hotel. Each of the forty-nine guest rooms has been decorated with great care, preserving a look that is generally, but not exclusively, Victorian with brass beds and marble-top bureaus in evidence. Wall coverings are usually gentle prints that are sometimes reflected in coordinated drapes. Every guest room has a private bath.

The public rooms carry through the feeling of elegance of the period with attractive chandeliers, wall-to-wall carpeting, and carefully laid tables in the dining rooms, each with fresh flowers and linen service. Drinks are served in the Red Parlor, a lounge that you enter through a doorway surmounted by a French Tiffany glass canopy. An unusual cast-iron fireplace adds a warm winter glow. The windows have been replaced with striking custom-made stained-glass window insets.

Dining is available in any of four handsome dining rooms, including the striking Gazeboe Room. Standing in the courtyard of the inn, the Gazeboe Room is a conservatory with a great domed roof that rolls back to reveal the sky on cloudless days or starlight nights. The inn offers a complete menu for each of the three meals plus brunch that are offered to the public and guests. At each there are always special offerings that distinguish the inn from more pedestrian restaurants. The regular breakfast menu is augmented by choices of eggs Benedict and a steak-and-eggs combination called Park Avenue. Dinner selections include a number of seafood choices such as poached salmon Hollandaise, sautéed abalone steak, or scampi; beef or veal choices such as stroganoff, beef Wellington, or veal Oscar; several poultry selections; and a number of items from the broiler. Dinners including soup of the day or salad, entrée, vegetable, potato or rice, and bread and butter generally range from $6.50 to $11.25. Appetizers and desserts are extra. *Room Rates*: All rooms are EP with rates ranging from $26 to $65 per night. *Pets*: Not permitted. *Driving Instructions*: The inn is in the center of Carmel-by-the-Sea.

SAN ANTONIO HOUSE

San Antonio Avenue between Ocean and 7th, Carmel-by-the-Sea, CA. Mailing address: P.O. Box 3683, Carmel, CA 93921. 408-624-4334. *Innkeepers*: Joan and Michael Cloran. Open all year. San Antonio House is an attractive turn-of-the-century home in a quiet residential area of Carmel. The house is surrounded by a tree-shaded lawn, flowering shrubs, gardens, flower-lined walks, and stone walls. There is even an ivy-covered garden wall with an arched gateway. Most of the house's seventy years were spent as a private residence until the 1950s, when it became the "Here We Go Again" Guest House, named for the owner's newspaper column. The inn

now welcomes guests into its warm, homey interior as the San Antonio House.

The Clorans are a young couple who in 1975 escaped to their beloved Carmel from busy city lives, Michael as a stockbroker and Joan as an interior decorator and art collector. They have thrown themselves wholeheartedly into the innkeeping adventure here. The five guest rooms are in two- and three-room suites, each with a private entrance. Each of these units is uniquely decorated with antique furniture, bright fabrics, rugs, and art from the Clorans' private collection. These guest quarters have painted wood-paneled walls and ceilings and sunny, open spaces lit by charming curtained windows looking out on pines and the gardens below. The "Doll House" is a three-bedroom suite at the top of the house with views of the ocean. The rooms have sloping ceilings and red-and-white checked gingham at the windows, matching the colors of the furnishings. One unit is a little cottage named "Skybird" with two bedrooms, two baths, a fully equipped kitchen, and a fireplace in the living room. All the guest suites have private baths, TV, and kitchenettes, their refrigerators stocked with orange juice and coffee makings. There are private patios and some fireplaces.

The Clorans provide a comfortable guest-house environment with complete privacy too. They serve no meals here, but that certainly presents no problem in Carmel. The town is just three blocks from the inn, and the ocean beach is even closer. On quiet evenings the roar of the nearby surf fills the air. The Clorans are assisted in their innkeeping by their able companion, Freddie, a black Labrador who greets guests and delivers their morning papers daily. *Room Rates*: Rooms range from $30 to $35 for two and are about $30 for a single, EP. *Pets*: Some well-behaved pets are permitted; check first. *Driving Instructions*: Carmel is two hours south of San Francisco off Highway 1. The San Antonio is on San Antonio Avenue between Ocean and 7th, three blocks from the center of town.

SEA VIEW INN

Camino Real, Carmel, CA. Mailing address: P.O. Box 4138, Carmel, CA 93921. 408-624-8778. *Innkeepers*: Marshall and Diane Hydorn. Open all year.

The Sea View is a two-and-a-half-story wood-shingled Victorian house that dates to the first decade of this century. There are a total of eight guest rooms, four with private bathrooms. Each room has its own personality, decorated by the Hydorns with a mixture of antique and near-antique pieces in a relaxed and attractive manner. The living room is a large, open, bright room in which a simple Continental breakfast of freshly baked muffins or coffee cake is served before the fireplace. Later in the day, the same room is often the gathering place for guests and the innkeepers to enjoy a glass of sherry together. Like so many small inns/guest houses, Sea View has made its local reputation by providing guests the personal services and attention that no larger hotel could. A private, secluded garden is available where guests may picnic or relax in the sun. *Room Rates*: Rooms with private bath range from $26 to $28, and rooms with shared bath are $20. Both rates include continental breakfast. *Pets*: Not permitted. *Children*: Young children are not encouraged but accepted "if well behaved." *Driving Instructions*: Take the Ocean Avenue exit into Carmel. Take Ocean Avenue to Camino Real, left on Camino Real 5½ blocks to the inn.

STONEHOUSE GUEST LODGE

Monte Verde and 8th Street, Carmel, CA. Mailing address: P.O. Box 2517, Carmel, CA 93921. 408-624-4569. *Innkeepers*: Barbara and Bryan Mosieur. Open all year.

"Stonehouse" is a fitting name. This attractive lodge has a completely stone exterior. Every stone is carefully fitted and mortared together

in a manner reminiscent of the stone houses of Pennsylvania. There is a striking star-shaped window above the entrance portico, and vines have begun to creep over parts of the house. The home was built in 1906, its stone hand-shaped by local Indians. Stonehouse was built for a certain Mrs. Foster, known locally as Nana. Mrs. Foster's grandfather had built the first Cliff House in San Francisco. Over the years, the guest register at Stonehouse has borne many names of the area's notables, including Jack London, Sinclair Lewis, Lola Montez, and Lotta Crabtree.

The interior contains an extensive collection of antiques. A fire burns nightly in the huge stone fireplace in the living room. The second floor contains six bedrooms, which share two bathrooms. The bedrooms have brass beds, down-filled pillows, and fresh flowers. The only meal served at Stonehouse is the Continental breakfast, served daily from 8 to 9 A.M. *Room Rates*: King-size rooms are $28.24, doubles $23.76, and singles $19.44. All prices include tax and breakfast. *Driving Instructions*: Take Ocean Avenue to Monte Verde, turn left, and go two blocks to 8th. Turn right, and the inn is the second house on the left, between Monte Verde and Casanova.

Columbia, California

Columbia, like many other California towns, grew up almost overnight following the discovery of gold on March 27, 1850, by Dr. Thaddeus Hildreth and his brother George. The town was called, by turns, Hildreth's Diggings, American Camp, and, finally, Columbia. By 1852, the town's population numbered many thousand and there were 150 stores, shops, saloons, and other enterprises. The abundance of lumber had encouraged its use in almost all construction and resulted in the town's virtual destruction by fire in 1854. Reconstruction was rapid, but so was another fire that destroyed the thirteen-block central business district in 1857. By 1859 the town had formed a volunteer fire department and had imported a quaint and fancifully decorated small fire engine, the *Papeete*. This was followed a year later by the purchase of a hand pumper, the *Monumental*. By 1860, most of the easily mined placer gold was gone, and the town began its gradual decline. In the next twenty years, many vacated buildings were torn down, and the population dropped from 10,000 to a few hundred. Luckily, though, the remaining structures survived, as did much of the early mining, firefighting, and other equipment unique to the Gold Rush days.

Today the town is part of Columbia State Historic Park. On display are numerous shops, stables, museums, and other early buildings that capture the spirit of days gone by. A tour of the village takes about an hour and a half by foot (cars are barred from the Main Street of the village to enhance the feeling of yesteryear). Special events in Columbia include the *Fire Muster* in May and the old fashioned *Fourth of July Celebration*. Also of note is the *Jumping Frog Jubilee* in nearby Angels Camp, held every May.

CITY HOTEL

Main Street, Columbia, CA. Mailing address: P.O. Box 1870, Columbia, CA 95310. 209-532-1479. *Innkeeper*: Vicky Shanklin-Bratten. Open all year except Christmas Eve and Christmas.

In 1856, in the midst of the gold fever that had followed the discovery of gold in Columbia, George Morgan began construction of the hotel that remains today a monument to that era. His two-story brick hotel, first known as the What Cheer House, was severely damaged in the disastrous fire on August 25, 1857. What Cheer was recorded as having incurred a $10,000 loss. Another fire in 1867 gutted the What Cheer, and Morgan waited until 1871 to rebuild the structure, then renamed the Morgan Hotel. In 1874 the name was again changed, this time to the City Hotel, a name it has borne to this day. In 1974, the building was completely restored and renovated with the use of

generous state and federal funds. It now serves as a gracious Victorian tourist hotel partially staffed by students receiving training in resort management at Columbia Junior College. Because the restoration and decoration of this impressive structure have been undertaken with public funding and because the hotel is managed on a nonprofit basis, the degree of excellence here is higher than would be possible at most privately owned hosteleries.

The two-story brick building with its wood and iron balconies and boardwalk only hints at the gracious interior and luxurious dining that await a visitor here. The public rooms have been restored with the warmth and quiet elegance (although not opulence) of the Victorian era. Walls are soft pastel tones accented by the warm glow of the dark wood trim.

Guest rooms (there are but nine) vary in size but not in the authenticity of their appointments. They include rooms with private balconies overlooking the tree-lined Main Street, parlor rooms that open directly onto the main sitting parlor, and the smaller but still ornately furnished hall rooms. Each room has its own toilet and running water in marble sinks. However, true to the Gold Rush era, bathing involves a short walk down the hall to the shower room. Each guest is provided a wicker basket containing a robe, slippers, and all the necessaries for a shower. Included in the room rate is a Continental breakfast of fresh juice, coffee, tea or hot chocolate, and freshly baked nut and fruit breads, muffins, and rolls. Guests frequently don their robes and enjoy breakfast in the parlor or bring their trays back to their rooms for breakfast in bed.

It is at dinner that the great advantages of eating at a fine cooking school become evident. The cooking takes place under the supervision of a French chef, and the meals are *haute cuisine*, but the supporting labor for his kitchen is provided by the aspiring chefs. The result is a particular attention to detail that might result in prohibitive labor costs in a commercial establishment. The choices for dining are a splendid cross-section of French artistry. Some of the appetizers include bay shrimp and avocado with sauce à la Horcher, Bluepoint oysters with shallots and vinegar, *coquilles St. Jacques*, and baked oysters with mushrooms and mornay sauce.

There are five vegetables and choices of twenty carefully prepared entrées. A sampler includes duck roasted with orange sauce; poached chicken à la Cynthia; fried trout meunière; braised sweetbreads; veal scallop with mushrooms, apples, and cream sauce; marinated hare; frog legs; stuffed loin of lamb Florentine; Chateaubriand with Béarnaise; three other steaks; and brochette of beef on skewers. Following this repast are six desserts to choose from for those hardy enough to continue eating. A meal for two that includes appetizer or soup, salad, vegetable, entrée, dessert, and coffee should run about $35 to $50, certainly not inexpensive, but within reason considering the care in preparation and quality of ingredients used. Much more modest and smaller samples of the cuisine are available at lunchtime. *Room Rates*: Rooms range from $33.50 for hall rooms to $42.50 for balcony suites. All rates are double occupancy. *Pets*: Not permitted. *Driving Instructions*: Columbia State Park is off Route 49. Main Street is closed to traffic during the day, but the hotel may be approached from a side street at those times.

Dinsmore, California

Dinsmore is a tiny one-horse town, one of the few remaining stage stops, in the heart of the redwood giants at the entrance to the vast Trinity Wilderness Area. Comprising no more than the Dinsmore Lodge with its restaurant and bar, a general store, and a service station, the town sits beside the Van Duzen River and can be reached on Highway 36, one of California's first state highways, with unbelievable scenery. The road winds through towering redwoods that were old at Christ's birth. Deer and an occasional bear will cross the road. On each side are wildflowers, old graying barns, and tiny one-lane bridges. There are rain forests of profusely growing ferns and hanging mosses and majestic mountain views of *Mount Shasta* and the *Trinity Alps* to the east. Trout fishing is excellent in the Van Duzen River. Nearby *Ruth Lake* offers lake fishing, boating, and water skiing in summer with complete rental services available. The lodge described below can supply hikers with Forest Service Maps of the Trinity and Six Rivers National Forest areas with their hundreds of miles of trails. This is reportedly "Bigfoot" country, so maybe you will catch a glimpse of the Yeti's American cousin.

DINSMORE LODGE

Highway 36, Dinsmore, CA 95526. 707-574-6466. *Innkeepers*: Mark Korkowski and Bill Hulse. Open all year.

Here in California's vast wilderness area of incredible beauty and solitude is the Dinsmore Lodge, a peaceful retreat far away from busy civilization. Nestled amid tall pines and oaks, the yellow and white porch-rimmed lodge sits surrounded by its own 475 acres with 2½ miles of the Van Duzen River running just behind it. The property lies in the Six Rivers National Forest and the Trinity Wilderness Area. Originally the site of a Wintoon Indian camp, the lodge was built at the turn of the century as a stagecoach stop.

Mark Korkowski and co-owner Bill Hulse spent years restoring the old lodge and buildings. The lodge is the center of the operation, but there are a total of twenty-seven cabins, guest houses, barns, outbuildings, and corrals. The old lodge is reminiscent of a stay at grandma's. The eight guest rooms are filled with period antiques from the old stagecoach days. In keeping with the flavor of the lodge are the shared hall baths. The guest houses provide six additional guest rooms, and there are six cabins, some on the palisades overlooking the river, where guests can rent by the week and must bring their our utensils. The guest cabins have been furnished and carpeted with more modern furnishings. The innkeepers own the restaurant across the road, where guests can get any of the three meals. There is also a bar. A special treat at Dinsmore is an evening barbecue with delicious, sizzling steaks or a nighttime cookout down by the river.

The Dinsmore Lodge is an authentic old-time resort, the kind with barns, corrals, and an unbelievable number of outdoor natural activities. Guests at the lodge who wish to stick close to home base can lounge in the big tree hammocks or go for a dip in the old swimming hole. A favorite pastime is to coast lazily down the Van Duzen River in a raft or an old inner tube. Be sure to bring old sneakers and clothes for traipsing in the river bed; the stones are beautiful, and you can take as many as you can carry. You can even try your hand at panning for gold.

In addition to the endless prospects for adventure in the surrounding wilderness, the innkeepers offer trapshooting, horseback riding, and guided tours of the countryside in their four-wheel-drive jeep. The river is full of delicious trout just waiting to be caught, so bring fishing gear. The Mad River is just over the hill in the lodge's jeep; here steelhead, salmon, and trout run six times a year. *Room Rates*: Main lodge rooms are $18 single, $22 double, and $28 twin doubles, MAP. The cabins and housekeeping rooms rent by the week; cabins range from $175 to $225 and rooms, $55 to $75 per person. *Pets*: Not permitted. *Driving Instructions*: Drive east from Highway 101 at Alton, 22 miles south of Eureka in Northern California. The lodge is 44 miles from Alton up its driveway (Route 36) through the redwoods. There is a county airstrip a block away from the lodge, so guests can charter a plane or fly themselves in.

Downieville, California

Downieville is a small community that serves as the county seat of Sierra County in the heart of the northern section of the Sierra Nevada Mountains. The town has a population of only 360, reflecting the very low population of the county. It is the low population and consequent abundance of virgin land that attract visitors to the region. The county as a whole contains about forty-five mile-high lakes and approximately 700 miles of trout streams. The eastern part of the county consists of the Sierra Valley, considered the finest farming and cattle ranching land in the state.

Route 49, the Gold Highway, traverses the county, along with Route 89. The contrast between the harshly rugged and beautiful Sierra Nevadas, often called the "Swiss Alps of America," and the gentle farmland makes a drive across the scenic Route 49 particularly pleasant. A fine stop along the way is at the *Kentucky Mine State Historic Park* in Sierra City, about halfway between Downieville and the lovely Yuba Pass to the east. Kentucky Mine is one of the few restored hard-rock gold mines and stamp mills. The best trout fishing is in the North Fork of the Yuba River, where both rainbows and German browns are stocked.

SIERRA SHANGRI-LA

Highway 49, Downieville, CA. Mailing address: P.O. Box 285, Downieville, CA 95936. 916-289-3455. *Innkeepers*: Kavin Hagstrom, Robert Bush, and George Hagstrom. Open all year.

Sierra Shangri-La is a group of eight cottages that cling to the edge of the Yuba River in the Sierra Nevada Range at an elevation of 3,100 feet. As such it does not qualify as an "inn," but its peaceful beauty in one of the most spectacular counties in the state, combined with its availability on a single-night stay basis, make it irresistible. Also irresistible are the surroundings. It was this very mountainside where Jim Crow and his renegades once looted the Mother Lode of its gold. Shangri-La is at the former site of the early mining camp known as Crow City. The cottages are at the base of Jim Crow Canyon and are shaded by Douglas fir, black oak, big-leaf maple, and red alder. Some cottages perch on the very edge of a tall wall made of carefully selected, smooth-worn riverbed stones. This wall divides the cottages from the woods and the racing river below. It was built after the flood of 1962 and is more than 1,800 feet long, averages 12 feet in height, and is about 7 feet thick at the base.

Each cottage has private bath with tile shower, completely equipped kitchen, deck, individual patio, and all bedding. Beyond that the cottages differ from each other somewhat. Three have Franklin stoves and the remainder have pot-bellied stoves. Most cottages are two-bedroom homes, except for "Jim Crow," a more remote and private cottage popular with honeymooning couples. High on the list of activities is fishing for both rainbow and German brown trout in the Yuba. Hiking in the woods and taking in the four-season beauty of this handsome place rank equally high for most visitors. *Room Rates*: Cottages range from $27 to $38 per day, double occupancy. Additional guests are $3.50 per day. Reservations are taken for weekly stays only from June through September. *Pets*: Not permitted. *Driving Instructions*: The cottages are 3 miles east of Downieville on Highway 49.

Elk, California

Elk is a tiny town of 500 people on the rugged Mendocino County coast. It sits high above the Pacific in a peaceful area of great beauty. Once a prosperous redwood lumbering town, its lumber tramways and schooner loading wharfs are now all gone. All that remains of the gigantic lumber business here are the old Victorian homes built to house the company executives and visiting VIPs from the East. The beaches with their tortured rock formations and water-worn caves are strewn with bleached and worn driftwood. The roots, trunks, and even little twigs are collector's delights. Rivers uproot the trees, which then are polished by the sea and eventually wash up along the coast. Secluded grottoes are perfect for sunbathing and swimming. The hills and cliffs rising from the beaches are criss-crossed with hiking trails. The town has plenty of old-time charm. For almost unlimited tourist attractions and good restaurants, Mendocino and Fort Bragg are to the north on the Coast Highway (see **Mendocino County**).

ELK COVE INN

P.O. Box 367, Elk, California 95432. 707-877-3321. *Innkeepers*: Hildrun-Uta and Michael Boynoff. Open all year.

Elk Cove Inn sits high on a bluff overlooking a rocky coast and the ever changing ocean. The small-scale Victorian mansion looks very European surrounded by old-fashioned flower gardens. A red clematis twists its way up the porch post, and flower-filled window boxes line the porch roof. The hills of the Mendocino coastline rise behind the inn, and a path winds down to the driftwood-strewn, secluded

beaches.   Elk Cove has its own private beaches lying under high, rocky cliffs.

The inn itself was built in the early 1880s by one of the area's largest lumber companies for its superintendent. The innkeeper, Hildrun-Uta, and her first husband fell in love with the place and spent eight months repairing, repainting, and redecorating. Two years later they purchased the lumber company's old redwood guest house three-quarters of a mile up the road. This too was polished and given a new lease on life as the "Sandpiper," where most of the guests are housed. Built in the early 1900s, it offers several guest rooms and a large, handsome living room complete with redwood beams, an enormous working fireplace, and an extensive library where guests can sit and relax. The Main House offers two guest rooms and houses the dining rooms, a big living room with fireplace, and the Boynoffs' living quarters. All the rooms in both houses are attractively decorated and are furnished with a comfortable mixture of antiques and near-antiques. Most of the guest bedrooms look out on the ocean, and two rooms have views of the gardens and hills behind the inn. There is also a two-bedroom cottage near the main house with scenic views, which rents as one unit. The inn accommodates about twelve to fourteen guests. The Boynoffs point out that there are no phones or color television sets here, and although guests might sleep on a comfortable queen-size bed, it will definitely not be a waterbed.

Guests all assemble in the main house for breakfasts and dinners. The meals here are a treat. Hildrun-Uta spent her childhood in Germany and later helped her mother with her catering business in Connecticut. Hildrun-Uta is an excellent cook whose specialties are of the German and French cuisines. She is now in the process of finding time in her busy schedule to complete a much-awaited cookbook featuring dishes from Elk Cove Inn. The dining rooms are open to guests for breakfast and dinner and to the public for dinner only. Some of Uta's specialties served here are sauerbraten, Konigsberger Klops (poached meatballs in a lemon-caper sauce), *Rouladen*, hasenpfeffer (rabbit in a sour cream sauce), *coq au vin rouge*, and *boeuf à la bourguignon*. For dessert one may choose from such delights as lemon Bavarian cream, *mousse au chocolat*, or orange buttercream torte. A good selection of wines and beers is available with the meals. There are freshly baked breads and fresh vegetables from the inn's garden. So many guests requested Uta's recipes that she had some printed up when she no longer had time to write them out. *Room Rates*: For two people including breakfast and dinner, rates are $68 to $74. *Pets*: Not permitted. *Children*: Under eight not permitted. *Driving Instructions*: The inn is four and a half hours up the coast from San Francisco on Route 1. The drive is only three and a half hours if you take Route 101 from San Francisco to Cloverdale, then Route 128 to the coast at Route 1, then left (south), five miles to Elk.

HARBOR HOUSE

Coast Highway 1, Elk, CA. Mailing address: Box 167, Elk CA 95432. 707-877-3202. *Innkeeper*: Patricia Corcoran. Open all year. Harbor House is a magnificent redwood estate built in the early 1900s to lodge visiting lumber company executives from the East. The inn has exquisite detailing everywhere. Its crowning glory is a large living room with vaulted, beamed ceiling, an enormous fireplace, and doorways and walls covered with redwood panels still perfectly preserved by a layer of beeswax that was hand-rubbed into it when the inn was built. Workmen painstakingly carved, fitted, and rubbed each piece.

The furnishings and décor throughout are of a splendor in keeping with the house. The innkeepers have re-created an Edwardian atmosphere with period antiques, overstuffed chairs, and well-stocked bookcases. There is a fine collection of old photographs of turn-of-the-century logging operations, showing the tramways and big lumber-carrying schooners. The inn has five guest rooms in the main house and four cottages (each a single unit) perched on the bluffs next to the inn. All the cottages are furnished with antiques and have Franklin stoves on brick hearths. The rooms have views of the ocean and the water-eroded rock formations below. Some of the cottages have private terraces. The inn's guest rooms have full-size fireplaces, antique furnishings, delicate floral wallpapers, and electric blankets on the fourposter beds. All have private baths.

Meals are served in traditional country inn style with one menu, plenty of delicious food, and a crackling fire in the fireplace. Not so traditional is the breathtaking view of the rugged coast from the windows. Breakfasts and dinners are served to the public with a day's advance reservation. Some of the inn's specialties are marinated ling cod, broiled salmon, Iberian pork chops, and beef macconaise. Two favorite desserts are mocha toffee pie and chocolate mousse pie. Everything here is fresh and made from scratch—from the soups to the hot, fragrant breads and rolls. The owners maintain a wine list that includes the best from the local wineries. They also serve a variety of beers and ales, but no hard liquor.

Room Rates: $65 to $85 for two, MAP. Rates are 15 percent lower in midweek. *Pets*: Allowed only in cottages. *Children*: Not permitted. *Driving Instructions*: Three hours from San Francisco on Route 101 to Cloverdale. From Cloverdale take Route 128 to Coast Highway, Route 1. Harbor House is then 6 miles to the south in Elk.

Fort Bragg, California (see Mendocino County)

CASA DEL NOYO INN

500 Casa del Noyo Drive, Fort Bragg, CA 95437. 707-964-9991.

Innkeeper: Marilyn Shoemaker. Open March through December. The Casa del Noyo Inn is a twin-gabled, shingled house that sits amid 2½ acres of tall cypress trees, lush shrubbery, and colorful flower gardens overlooking the Noyo River and a busy fishing village. The original section of the inn was built in 1868 but was extensively remodeled and enlarged in 1910 by an executive of the Union Lumber Company. The work was done with many fine woods available to him and his company that are not available today. The small inn has five guest rooms, all with private baths. They are fully carpeted and are furnished with rockers, antique chairs, and beds with heavy quilts. A bar downstairs reflects the nautical imagery of the harbor community. The dining room has built its reputation on fresh seafood brought in daily to the harbor by the busy commercial fleet berthed there. The price of the entrée includes soup, a crisp salad, fresh French bread, and a homemade dessert. The menu offers salmon, cod, and sole in season and is augmented with steaks, prime ribs, lamb shish kebab, veal scallopini, and stuffed chicken breasts. Dinners range from $6.25 to $11.95. Breakfast is served in the guest rooms or on the deck and consists of fresh fruit juice, a fruit bowl, freshly baked goods from the kitchen, and tea or coffee. *Room Rates*: Rooms are $40 to $45. *Driving Instructions*: Take Route 1 to Fort Bragg and turn on North Harbor Drive at the south end of the village. Then turn left on Casa del Noyo Drive.

COLONIAL INN

533 East Fir Street, Fort Bragg, CA 95437. Mailing address: P.O. Box 565, Fort Bragg, CA 95437. 707-964-9979. *Innkeepers:* Donald and Catherine Markham. Open all year except three weeks in October and two weeks in the spring.

Colonial Inn is an attractive gray house with crisp white trim. It is situated in a quiet residential section of Fort Bragg. The inn, built as a private home in the early 1900s, became a guest house in 1945. The grounds around the house are most pleasant, with a big lawn and tall palms. The Colonial is a favorite among international tourists and visiting congressmen. Guests here can make interesting friends from all corners of the world. Richard Nixon slept here as a young congressman.

The Markhams provide eight comfortable guest rooms, each with television and private bath. Two of the rooms have wood-burning fireplaces, and wood is supplied for them. All the rooms at the inn are carpeted, and furnishings are early California. The Markhams love plants, which can be found just about everywhere. Food is not served at the Colonial, but there are a number of good restaurants in the town and environs.

The innkeepers here at the Colonial Inn have made it a warm and charming place to use as a home base while exploring the beauty of the area. The Markhams can steer you to wild blackberry and huckleberry patches in season and know (but may not tell) the best spots to hunt mushrooms, and beachcombing is great any time of the year. *Room rates:* Rooms range from $20 to $35. The inn is very busy on weekends and holidays. *Pets:* Not permitted. *Driving Instructions:* The inn is four blocks from Route 1 in the residential area of Fort Bragg, at 533 East Fir Street.

THE GREY WHALE INN

615 North Main Street, Fort Bragg, CA 95437. 707-964-0640. *Innkeepers:* John and Colette Bailey. Open all year.

If you are in Fort Bragg at the right time of year, you can sit in the solarium atop the Grey Whale Inn and watch through binoculars the migration of the majestic mammals for which this inn is named. Built in 1915 by C. R. Johnson, founder of the Union Lumber Company, the building was originally the Redwood Coast Hospital. Johnson had great concern for the safety and health of his sawmill workers, and his hospital was well constructed. It was in continuous use until 1972. In 1974, the previous innkeepers purchased the old hospital and converted it into a gracious inn.

Furnishings range from antique to modern with unusual touches such as the use of the old surgical lights as lighting fixtures in some of the bedrooms. Several of the rooms have kitchens, one has a fireplace, and one an interior patio. Two penthouse rooms with sun-

deck overlook Fort Bragg and the ocean. Eleven of the thirteen guestrooms have private baths. One studio unit is being equipped with special facilities for persons in wheelchairs. Breakfast is presented on trays that guests take back to their rooms to enjoy. Planned for the near future are a special breakfast room, a television room, and another for games. The Grey Whale is just two blocks north of the Skunk Railway Depot and within easy walking distance of the restaurants and shops in the center of Fort Bragg. *Room Rates:* Rooms are $24 to $38 for two persons from March through October, slightly less in the cooler months. *Pets:* Not permitted. *Driving Instructions:* The inn is at the north end of Main Street (Route 1) in Fort Bragg.

French Gulch, California

French Gulch is a tiny old gold-mining town that remains much the same today as it was in the bawdy days of the miners. That is to say, it appears the same, but it is in truth a great deal more peaceful. At the gateway to the vast *Shasta-Trinity Alps Wilderness*, the town is surrounded by the steep Trinity Mountains and huge dammed lake reservoirs. A few vintage buildings remain on the main street alongside Clear Creek. There is the *French Gulch Hotel and Saloon*, and across the street is *Fox's Store*, the miners' supply store in the late nineteenth century. It has been in the same family for a century, and it still has the original mirrored oak bar, swinging doors, oiled slab floors, and penny-candy counters of yesteryear. Owner Don Fox has mining receipts and bills from the time when the mining companies ran up bills of up to $13,000, which would be paid off after a single cleaning of the sluices. *Saint Rose's Catholic Church* was built in the late nineteenth century, and once a month a traveling priest would come by. No services have been held there in more than twenty years, but the church is open to visitors. There are three old cemeteries around the town, just wonderful for poking about in to read the historic old tombstones. A Mrs. DePoister recently purchased the old schoolhouse, and she is restoring it to be her home and a store. The hills around the town are great for hiking and exploring, but hikers should be careful near the many deserted mines that dot the mountainsides.

Nearby Shasta is another old gold town. The *Shasta Historical Museum* is located in the *State Historic Park* on Route 299, beside the large Whiskeytown Lake. The museum is open all year from 10 A.M. to 5 P.M. except on Thanksgiving, Christmas, and New Year's Day. Within a short radius around the town of French Gulch are many many museums, *Shasta College,* the huge power dams of the Whiskeytown and Shasta lakes, the Sacramento, Pit, and McCloud rivers, historic state parks, wilderness areas, and other large lakes—all providing endless recreational & sightseeing opportunities.

FRENCH GULCH HOTEL

P.O. Drawer 6B, French Gulch, CA 96033. 916-359-2114. *Innkeepers:* Daniel Joe and Shirley Paulson. Open April 1 to December 31.

The French Gulch Hotel stands at the entrance to the beautiful Shasta-Trinity Alps, with their vast wilderness of high mountains and clear lakes. The old hotel and saloon were built at the height of the gold rush to cash in on some of the incredible wealth flowing out of the mountain mines: The average miner made between $100 and $200 a day in those years and spent it freely. The town and its hotel haven't changed much since the days when Black Bart held up the French Gulch stage.

The hotel was built by the Feeney family of Ireland. The old place has seen a lot of wear and tear, beginning with the rowdy miners and recommencing in the 1920s, when bootleggers made it

one of their favorite haunts. With these colorful characters came the inevitable "ladies of the evening" frequenting the lodgers' rooms. After the mines had closed and Prohibition had been repealed, the bawdy old hotel slipped into neglect and disrepair. In 1966, it was purchased and given a major facelift. An old bar was rescued from the extinct Empire Hotel and placed in the French Gulch's saloon. The bar has its own colorful history: It was built in England and placed on a square-rigged schooner for a rough trip across the Atlantic and around the Horn to San Francisco, where it was hoisted onto a horse-drawn wagon for an even more rugged journey up the coast to Oregon—where its purchasers refused delivery. It eventually ended up in French Gulch, a town literally in the middle of nowhere, and it remains there to this day, worn smooth by the many elbows and boots of the miners, bootleggers, and painted ladies of the past and the visitors of today.

The four guest rooms in the hotel are all furnished with the antiques of the miner's Old West. There are heavy oak bedsteads and dressers and period decorations and wallpapers. Some of the walls are of pecky cedar. The lodgings are on the ground floor and look out on the street. The sidewalk is shaded by an old white wooden balcony.

The dining room contains old oak furnishings, red-and-white checkered tablecloths, antique mining memorabilia, and period newspapers. The walls are covered with old lanterns, saws, picks, and other mining apparatus. Dinners are served family style. Soups come in big tureens, and the meals include fresh green salads, hot breads, and potatoes with the entrées. Steaks and ribs are the featured items, although there is a vegetarian plate and a shrimp scampi with prawns in a special wine sauce. The dessert is either ice cream or homemade bread pudding. On Sundays, the hotel offers a special brunch from 10 A.M. to 2 P.M.: For $3.95, diners get a choice of omelets, country fried potatoes, hot biscuits, country gravy, honey, and plenty of hot coffee in big mugs. The saloon serves liquor and wines. The restaurant is open only Thursday evening through Sunday evening for dinner. *Room Rates:* Rates are $25 a night. *Pets:* Not permitted. *Driving Instructions:* Take I-5 to Redding, then head west on Route 299W. Go approximately 10 miles past Whiskeytown Lake to the French Gulch turn-off. From there, go 3 miles up the gulch to French Gulch.

Georgetown, California

Georgetown is a simple, unpretentious village with a tourist trade that is modest compared to that of many other California villages. Many of the stores have covered boardwalks in front of them, and it is not unusual to see a horse tied out in front of one of the local bars. Shades of the old West. More out-of-towners than usual are present for the *Founders' Day Parade* and the *Jeepers Jamboree*, both held in August. The town comes alive with the bright yellow blooms of the omnipresent Scotch Broom every May. There are also many organized tourist events in Coloma, which is about 10 miles from Georgetown.

WOODSIDE MINE

Main and Orleans Street, Georgetown, CA. Mailing address: Box 43, Georgetown, CA 95634. *Innkeepers:* Al and Marion Podesta, Margie Whitelaw. 916-333-4499. Open all year.

Behind the wraparound two-story porch with its elaborate decorative corner brackets lies an interesting four-gable clapboard inn, actually a work in progress. Currently overseen by Marion Podesta, a charming and energetic woman who came to this country from her native Germany seventeen years ago, the inn has been the recipient of her painstaking renovations since the Podestas purchased the former

American Hotel in 1973. The building has been remarkably enduring, having survived three fires. The last one in 1899 almost destroyed the original building, and only fragments of the original structure survive in what is now called Woodside Mine. In the interim the building has been a rooming house and a sanitarium. It was the scene of many a late-night gambling foray by Lola Montez, a renowned "lady of the evening" of the earlier era.

As the rooms emerge, they are being furnished in an eclectic mix of period antiques. The rooms will have wainscoting, crown mouldings, and ornamental mopboards. Oriental rugs will be the rule, and queen-size beds will be adorned with dust ruffles, down pillow cases, and handsome bedcovers. Bathrobes will be provided as well. The floors throughout the inn, of particularly handsome red fir, have been thoroughly scraped and provided with coats of high-gloss varnish.

The downstairs, in its final form, will include a game room featuring the original gaming table used by Lola Montez. The adjoining breakfast room will have a Franklin stove, bay window, and French doors with a fanlight above. In warmer weather, the French doors will be thrown open to the terrace, where breakfast may be taken. Breakfast can also be enjoyed in the garden if guests prefer. There is a lovely Bonsai collection, and an abundance of herbs grow here, available for guests to take home when they leave, and an equal abundance of fresh fruit of all sorts. The *pièce de résistance* is the garden aviary with its seven pairs of wild North American ducks, snow geese, finches, and cockateels.

As a general rule, only breakfast is served at the inn. On occasion, Marion will cook a special gourmet dinner, served on tables that reflect the same attention to detail in the place settings as she has shown elsewhere in the house. Marion prides herself on never serving a guest the same breakfast twice during a stay. One morning will bring strawberry-filled German pancakes as the main dish, whereas another might feature Wesphalian ham or Canadian bacon, custom-made for her by her German butcher. On another day the breakfast might be built around bagels and lox. In any case, there are always fresh fruit, juices, and the hot beverage of choice.

Much of the discussion of the Woodside has employed the future tense, because the job of renovation is continuing. When we last checked, the downstairs guest room with private bath was being regularly rented, and others were soon to be finished upstairs. However, it is Marion's best guess that as much as two years more will be required to put the place exactly as she wants it. Call before going, and the Podestas will be happy to tell you what is available and whether there will be any disruptive renovation work under way during your visit. *Room Rates:* $40 for the downstairs room with private bathroom. Breakfast is included. *Pets and Children:* Children under thirteen years and pets not permitted. *Driving Instructions:* Georgetown is northeast of Sacramento. Take Route 49 to the town of Cool. Turn east on Route 193 and drive through Greenwood to Georgetown.

Gualala, California

Gualala is a coastal village at the northern tip of Sonoma County. The *Gualala Point County Park* there offers fishing, camping, and opportunities for nature study. For more area information see **Jenner, California.**

ST. ORRES

Highway 1, Gualala, CA. Mailing address: P.O. Box 523, Gualala, CA 95445. 707-884-3303. *Innkeeper:* Ted Black. Open all year except for part of March.

St. Orres, north of Gualala, is a remarkable building distinguished by twin Russian-style towers that rise more than 50 feet to their gleaming copper octagonal roofs. Each tower has an array of many-paned windows rising in ranks to a single row of spectacular stained-glass windows just below the copper crown. Between the towers is the main body of the inn with its heavy-beamed balcony, cedar exterior, and additional stained-glass windows set in a bank of oak doors.

When one thinks of California craftsmanship, one most certainly must think of wood, and it was with loving care that the builders of this inn slowly assembled the elaborate woodwork of both the interior and exterior. The walls of the rooms are faced with redwood carefully matched to form repeating designs. Where wood and contrasting rough plaster leave off, the details are carefully thought out and harmonizing. The quilts on the guest room beds are patchwork, some matching the wall panels in the intricacy of their construction. In-

deed, one could search for an entire stay here and not find a detail out of place, not one piece of wood hurriedly installed, as if time and money had made no difference to the builders. A crowning example of this splendor at any cost is the huge stone and brick fireplace in the lobby.

Upstairs are eight guestrooms, each of which shares one of three baths labeled "His," "Hers," and "Theirs." The food at St. Orres befits the elegance of its surroundings. One can start with *escargots de bourguignon*, a flaky Middle Eastern cheese and herb Tiropita, or even champagne and caviar for two ($25). There are salad choices and a soup of the day, then a choice of ten carefully prepared entrées such as *filet de boeuf au poivre vert*, scampi, sweetbreads *à la Forestière*, rack of lamb, abalone, sautéed chicken breast with mushrooms, shallots, and cream, bay scallops, and a daily vegetarian specialty. Entrée prices range from $5.95 to $12.95. *Room Rates:* Rooms are $35 and $45 and include a continental breakfast of fresh fruit, homemade pastries, and beverage. *Pets:* Not permitted. *Driving Instructions:* The inn is on Route 1, 2 miles north of Gualala.

Jenner, California

The *Stillwater Cove County Park* is 3½ miles north of Fort Ross and offers fishing, skin-diving, picnicking, and beachcombing. Of particular interest is the old *Fort Ross Schoolhouse*, adjacent to the inn that follows. The one-room schoolhouse was moved three times since it was built in 1885 and was in use until 1974. It is now restored in the period of its construction and is part of the county park. The *Fort Ross State Historical Monument* on Route 1 consists of a restored redwood stockade, commandant's house, and picturesque chapel. Founded in 1812 by Russians from Alaska, the fort was abandoned in 1841. It is open from 9 to 5 daily. Just north of Fort Ross is the *Kruse Rhododendron Reserve*. Lovely at all times of the year, the park is especially beautiful during the rhododendron flowering in April and May.

STILLWATER COVE RANCH

Jenner, CA 95450. 707-847-3227. *Innkeeper:* Linda Rudy. Open all year except Christmas Eve and Christmas Day.

Linda Rudy has converted the old Stillwater Cove Ranch into a charming collection of accommodations perched above the spectacular rocky cliffs of this coastal village. The ranch was first formed in 1931 as a private school for boys under the direction of Mr. and Mrs. Paul P. Rudy. Some fifty boys were boarded and educated in ranch life and academic subjects there for about thirty-five years. In 1966, Mrs. Rudy closed the school and began its conversion into a guest ranch.

The school consisted of a number of separate units, each designed to meet a particular school need, and the inn currently reflects these origins. There are separate cottages known as Teacher's Cottage and Cook's Cottage, as well as an East Room, West Room, King Room, and Dairy Barn. The last is a large bunkhouse with eight single beds, of interest to touring groups. All the units but the King Room have fireplaces, and wood is included in the price. Rooms are large, airy, and quite attractive. Cook's Cottage, for example, has exposed beams, a stone fireplace, wall-to-wall carpeting, and white wicker furniture.

At present, the inn does not offer meals to transient guests. It does, however, make its extensive kitchen facilities available to the many large groups (twenty-five to forty persons) that frequently book the facilities. Linda is a noted cook who, on special occasions, will do group family-style meals. Groups should inquire about this possibility. *Room Rates:* Rooms for two range from $20.00 to $32.50.

Bunk rooms are $60 per night for the eight beds, with extra cots available at $5 each. *Pets:* Permitted but not encouraged. A $2 charge is levied for each pet. *Driving Instructions:* The inn is 7 miles north of Jenner on Route 1.

Julian, California

Julian is the mother lode of Southern California. In its boom-town days, its population rivaled that of San Diego, and it was almost named the county seat in the 1880s. Local legend has it that the "flatlanders" from the San Diego area caused the defeat of the more mountainous Julian in the election to choose the county seat by giving all the miners so much to drink that they forgot to vote.

Today, visitors to the area enjoy the *Julian Museum*, open weekends and holidays from 10 to 4. The old *Eagle Mine* offers tours daily. There are a number of seasonal events of interest, including the *Wildflower Festival* held each spring since 1926 and the *Banjo and Fiddle Festival* (held since 1909), which brings flocks of musicians to compete in various contests and celebrates the apple, Julian's main fruit crop. The Banjo and Fiddle Festival is held the third weekend in September. There is also an autumn *Weed Festival*, which celebrates natural beauty through beautiful arrangements made of desert spoons, teasels, and sycamore buds. There is fishing at both *Lake Henshaw* and *Lake Cuyamaca*. The *Cuyacama State Park* offers hiking, camping, a horse camp, and an *Indian Museum*. *Anza-Borrego State Park* has camping and hiking trails.

JULIAN GOLD RUSH HOTEL

2032 Main Street, Julian, CA. Mailing address: P.O. Box 856, Julian, CA 92036. 714-765-0201. *Innkeepers:* Steve and Gig Ballinger. Open all year

The Julian Gold Rush Hotel is a charming inn with a Victorian flavor in a peaceful, unspoiled village. Gold was discovered in the village in 1870, and by 1880 it was a full-blown gold dust town, a sea of tents and shacks with, in its heyday, a total of fifteen hotels. One of them was the Hotel Robinson, later to be renamed the Julian Gold Rush Hotel.

The original name of the hotel dates to its initial construction by

a freed Georgia slave, Albert Robinson. He had come to the area originally with his former master, Major Chase. In time Robinson established himself as a cook and met and married Margaret Tull, also a cook. With a small capital advance from the major and their pooled savings, they opened a small but popular restaurant where Southern cooking and fine apple pie made with the excellent local apples were specialties of the house. Later the popularity of the restaurant prompted the Robinsons to expand their operation into a small hotel. They even managed to import two bathtubs, shipped all the way around the Horn, for their dusty miner guests. Gradually the clientele became more elegant. The hotel became the stopping place for the likes of Lady Bronston, the Scrippses, and the Whitneys. Many a young senator or congressman signed the guest register, making the hotel the "Queen of the Back Country."

Today, the hotel is maintained as it was at its Victorian supremacy. The rooms are furnished in antiques such as brass beds, 6-foot-high oak beds, and dressers. The walls have attractive Victorian wallpaper, and there are floral carpets and antique doilies. Most guest rooms still share the "necessary" rooms at the ends of the halls. The lobby has a wood-burning stove and comfortable chairs conveying an atmosphere of hospitality and warmth. The hotel is the oldest operating hotel in Southern California and was recently placed on the National Register of Historic Places.

In addition to the rooms in the main hotel there is a separate

Honeymoon House, which was built in the 1940s. It is a one-bedroom house with a wood-burning stove, wicker furniture, and lace curtains. No meals are served at the hotel. *Room Rates:* $14 to $28 per room. *Pets:* Not permitted. *Driving Instructions:* The town of Julian can be reached by Route 78-79.

Little River, California

Little River is a small village just to the south of Mendocino. For area information, see **Mendocino County.**

GLENDEVEN

8221 North Highway 1, Little River, CA 95456. 1-707-937-0083. *Innkeepers:* Jan and Janet deVries. Open all year except most of December.

Glendeven is a country guest house that has been fashioned from a Victorian farmhouse located 2 miles south of the bustling village of Mendocino. The rambling home was built in 1867 by Isaiah Stevens for his wife, Rebecca Coombs Stevens, and family. The large farm established by the Stevens family was renowned for the breeding of fine cattle and horses, skills brought to the Pacific Coast by Isaiah from his native Maine. His birthplace is reflected in the architecture of the house he built, typical of the New England feeling of the Mendocino area. Long afterward, after some years of the neglect brought on by the Depression of the 1930s, the house was purchased by Warren and Dora Zimmer, who did much of the restoration that is visible today. The house was finally purchased in 1977 by the deVrieses, who converted the property to its current use and renamed it Glendeven.

Today, the house contains an interesting and eclectic blend of fine antique furnishings (many European) accented with the DeVries' collection of modern ceramic pieces and paintings. Although this combination of styles is rather out of the ordinary, it seems to work in this house. The sitting room, also used for breakfast, has a working fireplace and a fine view of the open meadow and the bay at Little River through the bay window. There are six bedrooms. The Garden Room and the Garrett (at the very top of the house, under the eaves) have their own bathrooms, and their occupants are

served breakfast on trays delivered to the rooms if they wish. The remaining four rooms are on the second floor and share two baths. Each has a view to the south of the house.

Mendocino is filled with the hustle and bustle of a popular rural resort village. Staying at Glendeven, only 2 miles away, gives one the chance to have the proverbial cake and eat it too. After a day of exploring the shops of the village, it is pleasant to escape to the tranquillity of Little River and Glendeven. *Room Rates:* Rooms are $35 to $45 including breakfast for two. From January through March, the rates are $5 lower Sunday through Thursday. *Pets:* Not permitted. *Driving Instructions:* The guest house is on Highway 1, 2 miles south of Mendocino.

HERITAGE HOUSE

Highway 1, Little River, CA 95456. 707-937-5885. *Innkeeper:* L. D. Dennen. Open from February until the Sunday after Thanksgiving.

It is hard to imagine a more spectacular setting for an elegant resort inn than the surroundings of Heritage House. Perched on a rugged stretch of the Mendocino coastline, the inn is a collection of buildings that date back to 1877. The original farmhouse was constructed for the Pullen family by John Dennan, the grandfather of the current innkeeper. The site was first used for the shipping of hand-split redwood ties. The early farmhouse, reflecting the State of Maine architecture so prevalent in the Mendocino area thanks to its New England settlers, is now used as the resort's reception office, dining room, and kitchen. Over the years the property has served as a base for smuggling—liquor during Prohibition, and goods and people from the Orient—and as a hideout for the renowned bandit Baby Face Nelson. A secret cave used by smugglers is nearby.

Accommodations are mostly in a group of cottages tucked unobtrusively into the landscape. Most have been named after old-time buildings of note in the local area. Thus one may stay in "Scott's Opera House," the "Country Store," "Bonnet Shop," "Ice Cream Parlor," "Stable," and so forth. Many of the furnishings date from the mid-nineteenth century and have been collected over the years since the Dennans purchased the property. Many were made in the Mendocino area by local craftsmen, and others were imported by early settlers who brought them by ship around the Horn. Although many of the buildings have been erected in recent years, the care taken in construction and the use of materials and techniques compatible with the earlier period has resulted in a warm and comfortable place that seems rather ageless. One building, the Apple House Lounge, is an old apple storage barn that was dismantled on its site 24 miles away in Glen Blair and reassembled adjacent to the main farmhouse. The large stone fireplace, wideboard wall paneling, and sturdy beams add to the flavor of this popular gathering spot at Heritage House. The guest rooms are quite individual. Although there are some rooms in the main farmhouse, the great majority of the fifty-two rooms are in the cottages. One may choose from suites in the old water tower or cottages perched at the edge of the sea cliffs. There are private bathrooms in all rooms.

Meals are served in a long dining room bordered with a wall of windows overlooking the coastline. The menu here changes daily and offers a choice of two entrées. The two sample menus that follow represent a fraction of the offerings of this fine restaurant. In a full week, none of the main courses was repeated, and almost none of the accompaniments. One meal began with a turkey and noodle soup. The choice of entrée was between roast leg of lamb with sour cream sauce and marinated short ribs of beef. And a second meal offered French onion soup, pears and cheddar cheese with French dressing, and choice of corned beef with ginger glaze or sole with tomatoes. *Room Rates:* All rooms are MAP and range from $32 to $77 per person per day, depending on occupancy and room location and size. No credit cards are accepted. *Pets:* Not permitted. *Driving Instructions:* The inn is 12 miles south of Fort Bragg on Route 1.

LITTLE RIVER INN

Little River CA 95456. 707-937-5942. *Innkeeper:* Charles D. Hervilla. Open all year.

In 1853, a pioneer and lumbering tycoon named Silas Coombs built a rambling mansion in the style of his native Maine. The many-gabled roofline bears the icicle ornamentation typical of the Victorian period. Over the years the property has grown, and it has been operated since 1929 as an inn. The current innkeeper is the great-grandson of the couple who built the inn more than one hundred years ago. The property today consists of the original house with its office, parlor, bar, dining room, kitchen, and three attic bedrooms with ocean views. It is here that lovers of country inns are apt to be happiest. Also on the property are several cottages and a contemporary motel-type annex. Several of the cottage and annex rooms have wood-burning fireplaces. All fifty rooms have private bathrooms and ocean views.

The inn has a strong local reputation for fine food served to guests and public. All breads, soups, and desserts are homemade. House specialties include Swedish hotcakes, served daily at breakfast, and clam chowder, abalone, oysters, ling cod, and salmon served at dinner. The inn has a nine-hole golf course with PGA pro in attendance, open to the public as well as guests. Many of the trails of the Van Damme State Park are connected to the inn by footpaths. *Room Rates:* Double rooms range from $30 to $46, with suites as high as $80. *Driving Instructions:* The inn is 3 miles south of the village of Mendocino on Route 1.

Los Alamos, California

Los Alamos is a small village in central California, about 120 miles north of Los Angeles. A pleasant day's trip out of Los Alamos would include a stop at the *Firestone Winery* 8 miles to the south and then a tour of Solvang, 5 miles farther south. Solvang, the largest Danish town in the United States, offers the *Solvang Theaterfest* from July to September and *Danish Days* in September. Santa Maria, north of Los Alamos, has a *Performing Arts Center Theater* that is active from October to May, the *Elks Rodeo* in June, and the *County Fair* in July. In Los Alamos itself is the *Olden Days Festival* held every September.

1880 UNION HOTEL

362 Bell Street, Los Alamos, CA. Mailing address: P.O. Box 616, Los Alamos, CA 93340. 805- Los Alamos 2744 (dial Operator to request this number). *Innkeepers:* Dick and Teri Langdon. Open all year on Fridays, Saturdays, and Sundays only.

Dick Langdon, like many innkeepers we have met, is a refugee from the more hectic life of commerce. The head of a meat business in the early 1970s, he longed to change his life-style and immerse himself in a project that would use his energy and creativity. While touring central Cailfornia in 1972, he discovered the quaint town of Los Alamos and was soon introduced to the Union Hotel, then on the market. Although restoring a period hotel was far from his dreams at the time, he could not resist making an offer for the place. Suddenly the Union hotel was his whole life—his hobby, his home, his occupation.

The result is one of the finest hotel restorations in the country. Everywhere you look handsome antiques grace all the rooms, which have been reassembled by Dick and his resident master craftsman,

Jim Radhe. A hint of the monumental restoration task can be gleaned from a few statistics: 1,500 pieces of wood removed, stripped, sanded, and replaced; 750 pieces of brass fixtures removed and hand-cleaned; all floors scraped and repaired; and so on. The walls throughout the hotel bear excellent reproductions of turn-of-the-century wallpapers.

Dick recounts that his early days as hotel proprietor involved scouring the country for exactly the right accessories and furnishings. The hand-chiseled fireplace mantle came from an old Pasadena mansion, a pair of 200-year-old Egyptian-style burial urns were bought from a 92-year-old lady in Mobile, Alabama, and a desk lamp from the movie set of *Gone with the Wind*. As you enter the dining room you are greeted by an enormous grandfather clock set before the luxurious fringed swagging at the entrance to the room. The main dining room pieces, with their hand-carved lion's heads, all 100-year-old solid oak, were purchased from a Mississippi plantation. There is an old Western saloon that you enter through 125-year-old bar doors purchased from a bordello in the South. Upstairs is a parlor for overnight guests only. The walls are lined with bookshelves, and in the center of the room sits an 1880 Brunswick pool table overhung with a curved-glass Victorian hanging lamp that sheds a glow on the room.

The original hotel was built in 1880 but burned down in 1886. The old wooden structure was replaced with a "modern" building of 18-inch Indian adobe in the early 1900s. However, when Dick bought the place he discovered a picture of the old hotel as it looked in 1884, and he set out to restore the exterior to look exactly as it did then. To do this it was necessary for the crew to dismantle twelve barns, all more than fifty years old, for the wood to give the exterior the authentic look of the interior.

Dick has just purchased a 1917 four-seater touring bus, which he is having restored. The bus, originally made for Yellowstone National Park, will be used to take guests on tours to the wineries and to the Danish village of Solvang, nearby. The hotel's newly manicured Victorian "yard," when finished, will include a croquet course, horseshoe-pitching area, swimming area, badminton court, and Victorian gazebo for outdoor weddings. Eventually, Dick plans to provide turn-of-the-century costumes for overnight guests who wish to use the facilities of the yard.

Food here is simple, home-cooked, and served family style.

Although there is no particular menu, the dinner always includes cheese and crackers, homemade soup, tossed green salad with house dressing, cornbread and honey butter (a house specialty), country cooked chicken or platter of beef, potatoes, fresh vegetables, and choice of beverage. Fritters are served for dessert. Adults are charged $5.99, and youngsters (weighed at the door) are charged from $1.99 to $3.99 according to their weight. This makes the meal a bargain if your children are underweight. *Room Rates:* Ten of the twelve guest rooms upstairs share baths; two have private bathrooms. Rooms with shared bath are $25, and those with private bath are $35. *Pets and Children:* Not permitted, but children are welcome to dine in the restaurant. *Driving Instructions:* Take the Los Alamos turn-off from Route 101 (14 miles north of Buellton and Solvang or 17 miles South of Santa Maria).

Los Angeles, California

It is well outside the scope of this book to attempt to steer travelers to the myriad tourist activities in this enormous metropolis. However, it is well worth while for any prospective visitor to the nation's largest city to make inquiries in advance at Greater Los Angeles Visitor and Convention Bureau, office of Visitor Services, 505 South Flower Street, Level B, Los Angeles, CA 90071. The telephone number is 213-488-9100. This office is very helpful. Try to give an idea of your length of stay and the kind of assistance you need, including your interests (museums, zoos, children's activities, for example) so that it can be of the most service to you.

HOTEL BEL-AIR

701 Stone Canyon Road, Los Angeles, CA 90024. 213-472-1211. *Innkeeper:* James H. Checkman, Vice President. Open all year. Pardon this brief excursion into the lap of luxury, to this home away from home for the world's beautiful people. If one has cause to find oneself in the midst of greater Los Angeles, there is no happier way to spend the time than in one of the world's finest (and deservedly most popular) small hotels, the Bel-Air.

There is barely a hint that this *is* a hotel. The rows of Spanish arches surmounted by the red tile roof, the towers, the lake and its resident swans, and the extraordinary gardens—all combine to erase any hint of commercialism. Even the lobby is more properly called the living room. Sit for a while in the gazebo in the garden taking afternoon tea and soaking in the artistry of the flowerbeds. Repair to the comfort of your suite or room with its exquisite furnishings representing a mixture of traditional European styles. Twenty of the sixty-eight rooms have open fireplaces. There is a pool used the year round, and the dining room has its own fireplace in a beautiful rock setting with garden plantings all around it. The Bel-Air was originally the stables of Alphonzo Bell, founder of Bel-Air and early developer of the region in the 1920s. It is difficult to see any traces of the stable days in the magnificent hotel.

Dining at the Bel-Air is, like staying there, a leisurely pleasure. The menu is decidedly Continental in influence and remarkably extensive. There are dozens of choices here, enough to suit even the palate of a jaded member of royalty or a visiting movie star. Soups range from a jellied bouillon through onion soup to *petite marmite*. There are nineteen appetizers including Beluga caviar with its customary high tariff. The remaining choices are moderate in cost and are almost entirely seafood offerings: shrimp remoulade, smoked salmon, shrimp *à la maison*, cracked crab in mustard sauce, and linguine with clam sauce. The main courses include broad selections of fish and other seafood, poultry, beef, and veal. A tiny sampling of these would include whole dover sole, broiled salmon, frog legs, lobster thermidor, broiled whitefish, peppercorn steak, noisette of lamb, sweetbreads Marechale with asparagus, duckling Bigarade, curry of turkey, and at least two dozen more. Remarkably, the prices here are quite reasonable, especially considering the setting. Soups range from $1.85 to $2.50, appetizers hover around $5.00 for the most part, and entrees range from $8.50 to $13, with all vegetables an additional charge on the fully à la carte menu. Expect to pay about $25 per person for a typical dinner. *Room Rates:* Rooms range from $52 to $85 for single or double occupancy. Suites are from $100 to $265. *Pets:* Not permitted. *Driving Instructions:* Drive east from the San Diego Freeway on Sunset Boulevard to Stone Canyon Road.

Mendocino, California (see Mendocino County)

HILL HOUSE INN OF MENDOCINO

10711 Palette Drive, Mendocino, CA. Mailing address: P.O. Box 625, Mendocino, CA 95460. 707-937-0554. *Innkeepers:* Robert and Gert Permenter. Open all year.

While living in Mendocino, Monte Reed talked with many travelers who had no place to stay. Realizing that there was a shortage of accommodations, he purchased the Hill House property in 1972 and began planning. Over the next six years, he and his wife, Barbara, worked to obtain a California State Coastal Commission permit to build the inn. The result is a brand new Victorian inn overlooking the Mendocino Headland State Park, the coastline, and the Cabrillo Lighthouse. The Reeds consider the completed inn to be the first stage of their long-range plan, to be supplemented by a bar and restaurant at a later time.

The Reeds have managed to create an inn of moderate size (twenty-one rooms) that combines earlier construction techniques (many gables and dormers, scallop-edged shingles, bay windows) with such contemporary features as large single-pane windows, modern bathrooms, and color television. The TV sets have been cleverly concealed in Victorian-style cabinets.

The large guest rooms are all done in Victorian décor with velvet quilted bedspreads, brass headboards, marble-top nightstands, velvet rocking chairs, and oak tables. The Victorian feeling is carried through with print wallpapers, rugs, hurricane lamps, Victorian-style ceiling light fixtures, and large gold-framed mirrors and pictures. Each room has a private bath, including tub and shower. Some rooms have double sinks. One unit has a working fireplace with a velvet Victorian-style couch and marble-top coffee table. Fresh flowers are placed around the inn from its own garden daily, and there is a central courtyard that has an abundance of hanging as well as planted fuchsias, which are native to the area. A Continental breakfast is delivered to the rooms daily. All in all, Hill House is a pleasant compromise between the truly old and the unacceptably modern. *Room Rates:* Rooms range from $46 to $65 for single or double occupancy. *Pets:* Not permitted. *Children:* The innkeepers note that they are not well equipped to handle children but, on occasion, will accept them. *Driving Instructions:* The inn is in the center of Mendocino. Take Main Street to Lansing Street, make a right turn to Palette Drive, turn right on Palette, and the inn is the first building on the left side of the street.

JOSHUA GRINDLE INN

44800 Little Lake Road, Mendocino, CA. Mailing address: Box 647, Mendocino, CA 95460. 707-937-4143. *Innkeepers:* Bill and Gwen Jacobson. Open all year.

Like most of his fellow townsmen, Joshua Grindle was a transplanted New Englander. He arrived from Maine in 1869 to make his fortune in the fast-emerging redwood lumber business. And, like those of his fellow-workers, most of his energy was, at first, devoted to the effort of establishing his business rather than looking after his personal needs. It was not until 1879 that he chose a wife, one Alice Hills, and began construction of their house on a plot of land given to them by his bride's family. Sadly, Alice was not to see the house completed; she died in childbirth in early 1882. Her son survived, and Grindle continued to live in the house until his death in 1928. Not until 1967 did the house leave the hands of the Grindle descendants.

The inn comprises five guest accommodations, a parlor, and a dining room, all housed in a building clearly reflecting Joshua Grindle's New England heritage. The inn is filled with a pleasant collection of early American antiques from the seventeenth and eighteenth centuries. There are many etchings, oil paintings, and serigraphs. Each guest room has a private bath, and two have working fireplaces. The fireplaces are decorated with hand-made tiles manufactured in 1870 at Minton's Stoke-on-Trent, a factory in England. The tiles in the old library–guest room illustrate Aesop's Fables, and those in the parlor depict old English children's stories.

Guest rooms come in all sizes and shapes. Each of the five is decorated with an assortment of antiques, simply arranged, with a few accessory pieces complementing the main furniture. There are three early hand tools arranged on the wall in one room and four

matching pictures in another. Some of the beds are brass, one is a fourposter, and others are simpler. One room has sloping ceilings, and several have interesting combinations of distinctive wallpapers.

Breakfast is served in the dining room on a 10-foot, 6-inch pine harvest table that dates from about 1830. The meal itself is "English style," with homemade breads or muffins, boiled egg, fresh fruit, and coffee or tea. In the early evening many guests like to gather in the parlor to enjoy the fire, play the baby grand piano, read, have a game of backgammon or chess, or talk of the day's exploring. The inn provides cream sherry on the huntboard for the enjoyment of guests. *Room Rates:* Rooms with ocean view are $35, with fireplace $40. *Pets:* Not permitted. *Children:* Not encouraged. *Driving Instructions:* Take Route 101 north from San Francisco. Turn west on Route 128, just south of Cloverdale. This takes you out to the coast and Route 1. Go 12 miles north to Mendocino. The inn is on the corner of Route 1 and Little Lake.

THE MAC CALLUM HOUSE INN

740 Albion Street, Mendocino, CA. Mailing address: P.O. Box 206, Mendocino, CA 95460. 707-937-0289; restaurant: 707-937-5763. *Innkeepers:* Bill and Sue Norris. Open all year.

As you walk up the brick path and the broad steps bounded by tubs of flowering plants to the Mac Callum House Inn, a sounding whale, carved from a single log, guards the walk on your left. The front of the substantial Victorian mansion is dominated by an elaborate single eve centered over the door, which in turn is flanked by a multipaned sun parlor and a New England–style porch. The house was built as an extravagant wedding present for Daisy Mac Callum, who lived

there for more than forty-five years until her death in the early 1950s. Part of the warmth that emanates from the house comes from the many furnishings Daisy collected throughout her lifetime.

When the Norrises purchased the inn and its surrounding outbuildings in 1974, they set themselves the task of converting a comfortable country home into an equally comfortable inn. When they finished with the main house, they took on the barnlike carriage house, the old greenhouse, a garden gazebo, and a water tower, all of which have overnight accommodations. In all, there are twenty guest rooms, all but one of which share bathrooms. Each has its distinct flavor: One room is covered from stem to stern with redwood paneling and wainscoting; another has old-fashioned floral striped wallpaper; in still another, white wicker sets the theme.

A happy way to relax in the lengthening shadows of late afternoon is to sit in the filtered light of the sun parlor enjoying a cup of tea or a glass of wine. One may then move to a dining room after 6:00 to enjoy a satisfying meal prepared under the direction of Al Feifer and Tim Cannon, who look after the inn's restaurant. Al and Tim adhere to some of the simplest of rules: No cans ever enter their pantry, and only the freshest food is ever served. The dinner menu lists about ten items, which range in price from $6.95 to $12.95.

Each of the entrées comes with salad, bread and butter, a vegetable, and rice. Typical fare are spinach-and-cheese casserole, medallions of beef Bourdelaise, roast game hen, abalone, lemon veal, veal champignons, bouillabaisse, poached salmon with béarnaise sauce, and crepes Alexander (made with crabs, shrimps, and scallops sautéed with wine). Specials of the day augment the basic list and include red snapper, fillet of sole, or homemade linguine with clam sauce. For starters guests may choose between homemade French onion soup, Mac Callum House mushrooms, *escargots*, and oysters casino. There is a separate charge for appetizer or dessert. *Room Rates:* Rooms range from $34.50 to $54.50 including continental breakfast. Suites are $75. *Pets:* Not permitted. *Driving Instructions:* The Mac Callum House is in the center of the village.

MENDOCINO VILLAGE INN

Main Street, Mendocino, CA. Mailing address: Box 626, Mendocino, CA 95460. 707-937-0246. *Innkeepers:* Beverly and Sarah Sallinen. Open all year.

The Mendocino Village is a gambrel-roofed, wood-shingled inn. It was built in 1882 as a private home, and additional rooms were added one by one in the later years. The house was originally the home of Doctor William McCornack and was occupied for several decades by a succession of members of the medical profession. The interior is maintained in a charming fashion typical of the late nineteenth century. Each of the fourteen guest rooms is furnished in antiques, and six have working fireplaces for which wood is provided. A trail leads

from the inn to the beach. No meals are served at the inn, but Mendocino is known for an abundance of excellent restaurants. *Room Rates:* Rooms range from $17 for a first-floor double room with hall bath to $38 for a double room with parlor, private bath, and fireplace. *Pets:* Not permitted. *Driving Instructions:* Mendocino is reached by taking Route 1. The inn is on Main Street.

SEA GULL INN

P.O. Box 317, Mendocino, CA 95460. 707-937-5204. *Innkeeper:* David Herstle Jones. Open all year.

Sea Gull Inn is a charming white Victorian home in a secluded garden courtyard behind the popular Sea Gull Restaurant. It was a family residence from its construction in the 1880s to the early part of the twentieth century. Today many of the family members still visit as guests, including one who was born in the old house.

The inn is reached through a covered walkway. The courtyard has flowers most of the year. The ten guest rooms are simple and comfortable. There are no phones, television sets, or fireplaces—just quiet, reasonably priced rooms, each of which has a private bath or shower and its own gas furnace. The beds have electric blankets. Some of the rooms are large and spacious. One has its own kitchen. Guests have easy access to the Cellar Bar, upstairs in the Sea Gull Restaurant. The bar and its large outside deck overlook the mouth of the Big River.

The Sea Gull Restaurant has the look and feel of an old "downeast" Maine tavern, the sort of place where one might find salty New England sailors partaking of stout and dark rum. The restaurant and bar are popular with Mendocino residents. The house specialties here are large shrimp sautéed with mushrooms and herbs, a homemade chicken Kiev, and baked red snapper, Scandinavian style. *Room Rates:* Rooms vary from $18 to $24, although an enormous guest room may be as high as $40. The rates depend on size, location, and number of beds. *Pets:* Not permitted. *Driving Instructions:* The inn and restaurant are in the center of the town of Mendocino.

Mendocino County

The extraordinary riches of the vast redwood forests stretching inland from the Mendocino coast were first discovered in the mid-nineteenth century. The early settlers of the area, mostly men from New England, set about the task of building their mills and towns and had little time for women or worldly pleasures. After the towns were established, women were sent for and family life began. Today, the Mendocino area attracts visitors by the thousands in the warmer months and in lesser numbers in the somewhat harsher winter. The rugged shoreline with its rocky beaches, blue sea, surf, and sheltered harbors gives way to the hushed redwood forests. The area is dotted with beautiful houses in the style of Victorian New England. One can find weathered barns, gardens, galleries, parks, and museums.

The focus of a visit to the area will probably be the village of Mendocino. This lumber port, settled in 1852, is now an artists' and vacation colony. Among the more interesting sights in the village are the striking redwood sculpture atop *Masonic Hall*, the *Chinese Joss House* (temple) dating from 1855, and *Kelley House* (1861), headquarters for Mendocino Historical Research, Inc. The *Art Center* on Little Lake Street has seasonal shows and sponsors an Art Fair on Memorial Day and another in mid-August. The *Mendocino Tennis Club* has courts available for public use. One of the finest ways to explore the land around Mendocino in an unhurried way is to rent a canoe from *Catch A Canoe*. One can then explore the Big River from its mouth at the bay as far as 55 miles upstream. The people at Catch a Canoe will be glad to help you plan a trip so that the tides will carry you up and back for a peaceful and rather effortless trip in both directions.

Just south of Mendocino is *Van Damme State Park*. To the north is *Russian Gulch State Park*. Both offer picnicking, camping, and beach access areas for fishing and beachcombing. Both offer acres of lush woodland with numerous trails that run from the tidal pools of the coast to the ferny woodlands of the interior. Just north of Mendocino is Noyo Harbor, the home port of the Northern California fishing fleet. The port is crowded with sport fishermen during the salmon season, vying for limit catches. The adjoining village of Fort Bragg is considered by many to be the seat of redwood country. A relaxing way to introduce all family members to the redwoods is to take a ride on the *Skunk Railroad*, operated by California Western Railroad, a division of the Georgia-Pacific Railroad. The tourist may take a full-day ride on a 40-mile standard-gauge track that winds through the majestic forest, crossing a total of thirty-one bridges and trestles and two tunnels as it travels from Fort Bragg to Willits. Those who wish a shorter trip may take the half-day voyage to Northspur. Some trains are powered by diesel and some by steam locomotive. The telephone number is 707-964-6371.

The *Mendocino Coast Botanical Gardens* is a 47-acre wonderland of rhododendrons, begonias, fuchsias, lilies, ferns, and trails. The gardens sponsor a Rhododendron Show in April and May and a Dahlia Show in the summer and fall. They are open daily from 8:30 to 6:00 from April 1 to November 1. Admission is charged. For information call 707-964-4352.

For information about this area contact the Redwood Empire Association, 360 Post Street, San Francisco, CA 94108; the Fort Bragg–Mendocino Coast Chamber of Commerce, 332 North Main Street, Fort Bragg, CA 95437; and the Mendocino County Chamber of Commerce, Box 457, Laytonville, CA 95454.

Montecito, California

Rising beyond the village of Montecito are the rugged foothills of the Santa Ynez Mountains and the beautiful San Rafael Wilderness Area. There are many hiking areas and horseback riding opportunities here, and nearby Santa Barbara offers a great many recreational and sightseeing activities to toursts in the area. See **Santa Barbara** for more information.

SAN YSIDRO RANCH

900 San Ysidro Lane, Montecito, CA 93108. 805-969-5046. *Innkeeper:* James H. Lavenson. Open all year.

San Ysidro Ranch, a hideaway in the foothills of the San Ynez Mountains above Mentecito, is one of the oldest guest resorts in California, having opened to visitors in 1893. Originally the land was part of a Spanish land grant, and Mission Santa Barbara padres worked the ranch in the very early nineteenth century. The original adobe built by the padres in 1825 still stands at the ranch and is a museum. The ranch is named for Saint Isadore, patron saint of Madrid, who, according to legend, was so kind that the Lord sent him an angel to till his fields. That freed Isadore to tend the sick and the needy, hence the ranch's symbol, a plow and an angel.

Today there is little around this sumptuous retreat to remind one of the sick and needy, but San Ysidro offers plenty of pampering and attention to small kindnesses. Arriving guests are conveyed to their cottages in a golf cart to find their names already engraved on a wooden plaque outside their door. Each of the thirty-eight cottages and cottage rooms is in a glen hidden in foliage and flowers, which gives a feeling of seclusion. The cottages vary in shape and design, some with several guest rooms and others for a single unit, but all contain sitting rooms or bedroom lounges. Most of these cottages have porches with views of the mountains and ocean and contain one or more fireplaces, and often a kitchenette. The Forest Cottage, the most expensive of all, has many rooms and that newest of all necessities, the Jacuzzi.

All this pampering and luxury harken back to San Ysidro's star-studded life under Ronald Coleman's ownership until his death in 1958. The ranch was always (and still is) filled with the "glitterati" of the world, all seeking the peace and solitude offered here. Winston Churchill, Somerset Maugham, Sinclair Lewis, and Aldous Huxley were among those who came to write amid the peace of the hills. Artists, politicians, and stars of stage and screen were also among the guests. John and Jacqueline Kennedy honeymooned here. Vivien Leigh and Laurence Olivier married in one of the ranch's gardens; even the Cabots and Lodges visited.

Today guests still can receive absolute privacy if they wish; some choose never to emerge from their rooms, which is possible thanks to the thorough room service offered by the ranch. For more social guests there is the Hacienda Room in the main lounge, with game tables, comfortable couches and chairs, a big stone fireplace, and an "honor bar" where guests pour their own liquor and keep track of the tab. The Plow and Angel is the ranch's bar, housed in the 1850s wine cellar. It features live entertainment and dancing in a low beamed-ceiling room lit by the warm glow of many candles.

Above the bar is the fine restaurant formerly a citrus-packing house. The dining rooms are separated by thick stone walls with archways hewn into them. The ceilings are high with exposed timbers. Fresh flowers, the antiques, and soft candlelight create an atmosphere of elegance. The menu features both hearty Western fare, such as juicy, sizzling steaks, and *haute cuisine,* the specialty being Wisconsin veal served in a variety of unusual ways. One favorite dish here is fresh artichoke hearts with prawns in light mustard sauce. Some of the country's finest chefs are often guests at the ranch and regularly visit its fine kitchen. The restaurant and bar are open to the public for all meals.

As one of the area's finest resorts, San Ysidro offers plentiful recreational opportunities. There are a heated pool, tennis courts with distracting vistas of rugged mountains and the blue Pacific, a stable full of fine quarter horses, and more than 500 acres of trail-crossed wilderness. If guests arrive with Fido and Old Paint in tow, these four-legged companions will be royally cared for (see *"Pets,"* below). *Room Rates:* Rooms range from $64 to $98 for two, EP. Cottage suites go from $98 to $129, and individual cottages (up to four bedrooms) go from $108 to "Infinity," all EP, double occupancy. *Pets:* "Well-behaved" pets are $3 a night (EP); horses are $12 a night (AP) and are served "gourmet hay." *Driving Instructions:* Take Route 101 for 5 miles south of Santa Barbara to the San Ysidro Road exit. Head toward mountains on San Ysidro Road for 2 miles. Take fork to the right at San Ysidro Lane, which ends at the ranch.

Monterey, California

Monterey is today an artist colony with many small antique shops and galleries crammed into the former canneries made famous by some of John Steinbeck's novels. Monterey is an important stop for visitors to the Monterey Peninsula. The famed *17 Mile Drive* is an easy way to experience the majesty of the ocean front and to scent the wealth hidden behind the gates to the fashionable homes of the area. The drive is circular and may be entered off Route 1 near the Del Monte Shopping Center or near Route 68 in Pacific Grove. The trip takes one through pine forests and groves of Monterey cypress, past some of the country's most famous golf courses (Pebble Beach and Cypress Point, among others). Deer frequently graze on the courses, and sea lions, sea otters, and migrating gray whales are frequently sighted in the ocean. A toll is charged for the road.

Monterey has many important historic houses and sights. Many of them are connected by an orange line painted on the streets to guide visitors on foot from place to place. One important stop on the orange line tour is at the *Royal Presido Chapel* (1795) at San Carlos

Cathedral on Church Street. The *Allen Knight Maritime Museum* contains collections relating to the fishing and whaling days in Monterey—ship models, steering wheels, bells, compasses, lanterns, scrimshaw, and navigation instruments. The *Monterey State Historical Park* is a collection of buildings spotted throughout the town and maintained by the state. Included is a home briefly occupied by Robert Louis Stevenson. The *Colton Hall Museum* and the *Old Monterey Jail* are housed in the same building, and admission to both is free. *Casa Amesti* is a colonial adobe structure with redwood trim built between 1834 and 1853. The house, at 516 Polk Street, was fully restored in the early part of this century and is open to the public on weekends. Admission is charged. For information about these and many other sights in the town, contact the Monterey Peninsula Chamber of Commerce and Convention Bureau, P.O. Box 1770, Monterey, CA 93940, or call 408-375-2252. For other area information, see the section on **Carmel, California.**

OLD MONTEREY INN

500 Martin Street, Monterey, CA 93940. 408-375-8284. *Innkeepers:* Ann and Gene Swett. Open all year.

The Old Monterey is an English country home with, as Ann puts it, "Tudor and Gothic manifestations." The ivy-covered building is surrounded by carefully landscaped gardens, enhancing the English feeling of the inn, recently converted from use by the innkeepers as

their country home. The handsome building with its many small-paned windows was built in 1920 by Carmel Martin, a former mayor and civic-minded citizen of Monterey. The home has been selected for inclusion in the National Registry of Historic Homes.

The bed-and-breakfast inn has retained all the warmth and home-like qualities that the Swetts put into the house over the ten-plus years they have owned it. The living room sets the tone for the whole house. A rich Oriental rug covers most of the floor, and the room is noted for the simplicity of its decorations. Several family pictures and an elaborate candelabra lighting fixture grace the otherwise un-adorned walls. A fire glows in a fireplace surrounded by several comfortable chairs and a sofa. At one end of the room, an antique pool table awaits the pleasure of the guests. This is clearly a home where one can be immediately at ease. There are seven guest rooms. Each bears a name, often indicative of a function or location. Library, for example has its own fireplace, a king-size bed, and bookshelves flanking the double windows. As is frequently the case, the floral print of the puffy European goose-down comforter is carried out in the curtains swagging a second pair of windows. The bed in Creek-side hangs from four chains, a trend that has spread through this state, we believe, from the inn at Sutter Creek. Beds throughout the inn are oversize, each with a luxurious comforter that engulfs you in warmth. Treetop and Bay View are the newest rooms at the inn, fashioned out of the former attic. Both include fireplaces, skylights, and private bathrooms.

Breakfast (juice, fruit, pastries, and coffee) is served in a hand-some dining room at a communal eight-foot table set on a fine old Oriental rug. An antique breakfront graces one end of the room, and the morning sun streams in through a bank of windows. The only other food and drink offered at this bed-and-breakfast inn are the complimentary wine and cheese, served to guests in the late after-noon. Incidentally, those who wish may have breakfast in bed. *Room Rates:* Rooms with breakfast are $55 to $65. *Pets, Cigars, and Children Under Sixteen:* Not permitted. *Driving Instructions:* Upon entering downtown Monterey, proceed south on Pacific Street, passing the library. The next street on the right is Martin Street. Turn right and go one long block to the inn.

Murphys, California

Murphys, on Route 4 about 9 miles from the Gold Highway (Route 49), is a perfect stopping place for the exploration of Stanislaus National Forest and the sequoias in the *Calaveras Big Trees State Park*. Also nearby are the *Mercer Caverns* and the *Moaning Caves*. If you do not plan an overnight visit to *Columbia State Historical Park*, this village is near enough to provide a convenient day's trip to the restored historic village.

MURPHYS HOTEL

P.O. Box 329, Murphys, CA 95247. 209-728-3454. *Innkeeper:* Barry Cannon. Open all year.

Murphys Hotel is a classic old Western mining hotel complete with a "Wild West" saloon. The Queen of the Sierra," as the hotel was first called, was built in 1855–56 by James Sperry and John Perry to accommodate visitors from all over the world who came to see the newest local tourist attraction: the Calaveras Grove of Big Trees.

The hotel was obviously quite elegant in its day, and it remains virtually unchanged by the ravages of time—although one rather severe ravage, a devastating fire, destroyed most of the town and the hotel's "fireproof" interior. The fire occurred in 1859, a few years after the hotel's opening; after almost two years of restoration, the hotel reopened—with improved fireproofing. In 1978, nine dedi-

cated admirers purchased the old place and hired a historian to help them restore it. Many of its rooms had been closed off, and the lobby needed a complete overhaul. The historian interviewed old-timers in the town and former guests in an attempt to gather as many details as possible for an authentic restoration to be completed in the spring of 1979. The old furnishings and decorations are still here, and the needed replacements come from the same period—the middle and late nineteenth century.

There are thirty-two guest rooms, but only nine are in the old hotel itself; the rest are in an adjoining motel, which has also been refurbished. The rooms in the hotel are much the same as they were in Sperry and Perry's innkeeping days: The baths are still down the halls, and there is nary a phone or television to be found in the place. President Ulysses S. Grant wouldn't notice anything unusual in his Presidential Suite today—it's just the way he left it. This historic building has been host to a great many notable or notorious guests including the above-mentioned president, Mark Twain, Henry Ward Beecher, Sir Thomas Lipton of tea-bag fame, Horatio Alger, Jr., John Jacob Astor, and the infamous gentleman bandit C. E. Dalton—alias "Black Bart." These interesting names and more are scrawled in the old registry on the worn lobby desk. Murphys Hotel has been used over the years as an authentic set in many Western movies, and its own history is just about as colorful.

The dining room serves three meals a day to lodgers, tourists, and townspeople. Drinks are served as they used to be, in the saloon in the next room. Breakfast is a hearty affair fit to prepare one for a long day in the mines. The specialty is flapjacks, supplemented by homemade jams, jellies, and fresh hot breads. The evening menu features steaks and fresh seafood. *Room Rates:* In the old hotel, rooms are $16.90 per person and the Presidential Suite is $20.08; motel rooms are $21.14 per person (EP). *Pets:* Not permitted. *Driving Instructions:* North of Sonora, turn off Route 49 at Angel's Camp onto Route 4 heading northeast into the national forest. Murphys Hotel is on Main Street (Route 4) in Murphys.

Nevada City, California

Nevada City was once the crowning glory of the region of the northern-California gold mines. Visitors to the town travel through some of America's most beautiful country. The *Empire Mine*, the longest operating mine in the state, is open to tourists, as is the estate of the mine's original owner. There are displays of mining history, mining equipment, and the mine shaft as well as the mansion of the owner, all on parklike grounds.

The *Nevada City Community Park* has a large swimming pool and tennis courts. On Father's Day the town holds annual bike races. Just below Red Castle Inn is the starting point of an annual *Raft Race*. *Nevada City Theater*, the oldest in California, hosts many musical and dramatic productions. The *American Victorian Museum* is housed in the historic Miners Foundry, built in 1856. This museum is dedicated exclusively to collecting and exhibiting art, crafts, and artifacts of the Victorian Period (1840–1900). A *Christmas Trade Fair* is held here for three days following Thanksgiving.

The village is noted for its many Victorian buildings dating back to the Gold Rush. Operating gold mines are within 35 miles of town, and skiing in the Sierras is less than an hour away. By far the most popular activity in Nevada City is panning for that elusive yellow metal, so bring your pans.

NATIONAL HOTEL

211 Broad Street, Nevada City, CA 95959. 916-265-4551. *Innkeepers*: Nan and Dick Ness. Open all year.

Nevada City was "Queen of the Northern Mines" in the bawdy days of the Gold Rush. The hub of most of the wheeling and dealing in those days was the grand old National Hotel, built in 1854 of bricks fired in the owner's brother's gold-mine kiln. Today the hotel, listed in the National Registry of Historic Places, is the oldest operating hostelry west of the Rockies. In its early days, the hotel was the headquarters of the Wells Fargo Express Company, whose stagecoaches made frequent stops here.

The hotel retains the charm and elegance of that colorful Victorian era. The trappings are all still here. Dick and Nan Ness have maintained the old place perfectly. Everywhere one is reminded of the plush, carefree nineteenth century. The public rooms and guest rooms are all completely decorated with Victorian antiques, period floral wallpapers, soft red carpets, chandeliers, and velvet and satin love seats and chairs. The parlor-lounge contains an old square grand piano whose history includes a trip around the Horn on an old schooner. The old hotel clock with its giant pendulum still ticks in its corner.

The thirty guest rooms all have furnishings of the period. In the five rooms with adjoining sitting rooms there are velvet cushioned love seats and marble-top dressers and end tables. All the rooms have luxurious beds, but some of the best are great canopied affairs with flower-print drapes and dust ruffles and white crocheted spreads. Twenty-five of the rooms have private baths. Some open onto the long veranda that spreads across the front of the hotel. The veranda overlooks an old-fashioned walkway below. In summer, cocktails are served at the tables here.

The cocktail lounge inside boasts a famous ornate bar, once the buffet in the Spreckles Sugar Mansion on San Francisco's Nob Hill. The dining room is open to the public for lunch and dinner. The tables there are lighted by coal oil lamps and red glass chandeliers. The walls are covered with formal wallpaper, old photos and portraits, and large plants. The menu features many veal dishes, prime ribs, and flambé steaks. Dinners come with a relish tray, soup du jour, tossed garden greens, pasta with sauce, potatoes, freshly baked breads, and coffee or tea. Prices range from $6.50 for a fresh fillet of sole or poached salmon to $10 for steak au poivre prepared at the table. Desserts are extra: cherries jubilee for two is $4.00, and crêpes Suzette for two is $5.50. Nan and Dick opened an antique shop in the hotel—the perfect place to browse before or after a hearty meal. There is a swimming pool for guests' enjoyment in summer. *Room Rates:* Suites range from $25 to $35 and regular rooms from $20 to $23 plus tax. *Pets:* Not permitted. *Driving Instructions:* Nevada City is 3 miles from Grass Valley on Route 49.

RED CASTLE INN

109 Prospect Street, Nevada City, CA 95959. 916-265-5135. *Innkeepers:* Jerry Ames and Chris Dickman. Open all year except for a short vacation in January.

The Red Castle Inn is an extraordinary testimony to the gingerbread "baker's" art. Built in 1857, the four-story Gothic revival brick building has row after row of verandas and porches with elaborate balconies. The roof line and gables are decorated with a continuous row of carved wooden icicles to complete the "frosting" on the cake. The

effect of all this is heightened by its position high on Prospect Hill overlooking the historic mining town of Nevada City.

Even though the Red Castle Inn is old by Western standards, it has managed to avoid the modernizing hand. Indeed, here the restoration has been quite faithful, from the original pine floors to the ceiling moldings. The building has been changed very little since Judge John Williams built it as a castle symbolizing the wealth he had amassed through a series of gold strikes dating back to 1849. The eight guest rooms here (six have private baths, an appreciated modernization) are furnished in Victorian antiques. There is a comfortable parlor for guests to use, as well as a series of terraced gardens and a pond on the property. Two of the guest rooms are made up into small suites that have a small bedroom and a sitting room with a working wood stove. Wood is furnished, and the evening fires make these rooms especially cozy in the cooler weather. No meals are served except a continental breakfast. *Room Rates:* Rooms are $25 to $30, year round, including continental breakfast. *Pets and Children:* Not permitted. *Driving Instructions:* Nevada City is reached by the Gold Country Highway, Route 49. I-80 serves this general area.

Occidental, California

Occidental is a former lumber town with about 100 people. It is set deep in a valley surrounded by high, rugged hills of redwood forests that extend far up the coast. The beautiful scenery of these hills and trees beckons hikers and lovers of peace and quiet. For aficionados of pasta and other Italian specialties, the town boasts three competing Italian restaurants. There are several antique shops in town, one in the Blackberry Inn mentioned below. Auctions are held here occasionally. The next town is Freestone, an untouched little hamlet that is definitely worth exploring. The rugged coast is about 10 miles away and offers party boats for fishing in Bodega Bay and rock fishing and clamming at Dillon's Beach. For more area information, see **Jenner, California** and **Sonoma, California.**

BLACKBERRY INN

3657 Church Street, Occidental, CA. Mailing address: P.O. Box 266, Occidental, CA 95465. 707-874-3023. *Innkeeper:* Charles Tomka, Jr. Open all year.

The Blackberry Inn is a small Victorian gem in Occidental, an old lumber town nestled in a gorge surrounded by towering redwoods and steep, rugged hills. The inn has been totally restored by Charles Tomka, Jr., its young owner, who loved the challenge of tackling the old house and in addition needed a place to show off his many an-

tiques. The house has lots of gingerbread trim on its eaves, porches, and tiny balconies. It is built on the side of a steep hill on the town's only side street. The ground-floor French doors open from the street into the Blackberry Inn Antique Shop. A curving staircase leads from the street up the hill to the main floor porch and entrance.

The house is one of Occidental's original homes, built in the early 1860s by a redwood lumberman named Meeker for his crew at Camp Meeker. Since its early days, the house has seen a great many tenants, but never before as an inn. In 1976 Charles started the enormous task of restoration. The effort has been well rewarded with a cozy inn in a peaceful setting.

The rooms are decorated throughout with Victorian antiques of the locale, stained-glass windows, plants, and many of the innkeeper's Persian rugs. The walls are covered with copies of period wallpapers accented with bright white moldings and trim. There are two working fireplaces, one in the plant-filled living room, and the other in the inn's only suite of guest rooms, the Blue Angel, with its Victorian furnishings and private bath. A custom-made stained-glass mural of a blue angel presides over the rooms. The other seven guest rooms share three bathrooms with claw-footed tubs, brass fixtures, and even old-fashioned oak toilets. But the most popular bathroom is the romantic lovers' bathroom in the suite, with its large sunken tiled tub for two. It has double sinks and showerheads, too. The bedrooms contain comfortable antique beds of brass, oak, or scrolly iron, covered with bright patchwork quilts. Most rooms have French doors, which open onto balconies overlooking the town of Occidental.

Continental breakfasts are served in the cheery dining room on the main floor: fresh French pastries, fruits, pots of homemade jams, and herb teas. Be sure to visit the kitchen, where the innkeeper's collection of blue china is displayed and where you'll find more of the stained-glass windows. Charles also provides guests with complimentary wines from the local wineries. For other meals there are three popular Italian restaurants. *Room Rates:* Rates range from $38 to $50. *Children and Pets:* Not permitted. *Driving Instructions:* Occidental is 10 to 12 miles inland from the rugged coast. From Jenner go inland on Route 116 and then south through Camp Meeker to Occidental. From Santa Rosa to the east, follow signs to Freestone and then to Occidental. The way is well marked.

Pacific Grove, California

Pacific Grove was originally called the Pacific Grove Retreat. During the summer a Chautauqua was held by the local Methodist Church there. Throughout the town, no drinking, smoking or dancing was permitted. As a further assurance that only the chosen would be able to come to the village, it was completely fenced in during an early period of its history. In time the moral restrictions have been relaxed, and the fence is long down.

Pacific Grove is only a stone's throw from Monterey's Cannery Row and the famed golf course at Pebble Beach, but it offers a quiet respite from the hectic tourism of those nearby areas. Tourists are drawn here for the several village festivals held annually. Most noteworthy are the summer *Festival of Lanterns*, the old-fashioned *Good Old Days* festival in March, and the *Butterfly Parade* in mid-October, which celebrates the wintering in Pacific Grove of millions upon millions of monarch butterflies. For further information, see **Carmel, California** and **Monterey, California.**

THE GOSBY HOUSE INN

643 Lighthouse Avenue, Pacific Grove, CA 93950. 408-375-1287.
Innkeeper: William Patterson. Open all year.

The Gosby House Inn is a solid Victorian mansion that was built in stages, beginning about 1886. During the early years, Mr. Gosby made it a practice to add something new on the house every winter. The Queen Anne tower that dominates the corner of the house today is one such addition. The earliest visitors to the Gosby House were members of the Methodist Church who came to Pacific Grove in the summer on retreat.

The restoration of both the interior and the exterior of the house has been done with particular care, resulting in one of the finer Victorian restorations of the West Coast. Each of the seventeen rooms is furnished with antiques and has a wash basin with brass faucets. The parlor, where the continental breakfast is served, is adorned with an antique doll collection. Two of its more special accommodations are the Gosby Suite with two double beds, private bath, and gas fireplace and the Steinbeck Room in the tower, offering its unusual shape and a fine view of the bay. Throughout the mansion, the original stained glass and wooden moldings have been carefully preserved.

Pacific Grove was originally a retreat from the more hectic life in the urban centers of California. Its summer breezes off the Pacific cooled those who came for relief during the Victorian period. Visitors today will find the same refreshing summer weather ready to greet them. *Room Rates:* Rooms are $26 to $36. *Pets:* Not permitted. *Driving Instructions:* Take Route 1 to the Pebble Beach–17 Mile Drive turnoff. Turn right onto Route 68 and follow the scenic route into Pacific Grove. Continue to Lighthouse Avenue, turn left, and go three blocks to the Gosby House Inn.

Palm Springs, California

For generations, Palm Springs was an exclusive watering hole for the celebrated, including every president since Hoover. Today the aura of exclusivity has worn off as the coming of the average American has swelled the annual visitor count to almost 2 million. Most of these visitors come to enjoy the recreational opportunities offered by the area. Palm Springs now boasts thirty-four golf courses, more than two hundred public and private tennis courts, and more than five thousand swimming pools. There are also three riding stables, an equal number of city parks, and more than twenty canyons to explore, the most famous being *Palm Canyon*, where more than five miles of palm trees have been individually illuminated. An eighty-passenger *aerial tramway* carries visitors from the warm desert to the 8,516-foot level of Mount San Jacinto. The tramway is open all year except for a brief vacation period in August. Admission is charged. The top of the tramway is the gateway to the 13,000-acre *Mount San*

Jacinto Wilderness State Park, with its fifty-plus miles of hiking trails and eleven campgrounds. The *Palm Springs Desert Museum* is a multimillion-dollar museum devoted to the ecology and folk art of the surrounding desert. Located at 101 Museum Drive, it is open all year. Admission is charged.

INGLESIDE INN AND MELVYN'S RESTAURANT

200 West Ramon Road, Palm Springs, CA 92262. 714-325-0046 and 714-325-1366. *Innkeeper:* Melvyn Haber. Open all year.

The Ingleside is a posh luxury inn consisting of twenty-eight accommodations that range from double rooms through mini-suites and penthouses to villas. You don't need a Rolls-Royce to make your entrance here, but you will certainly not feel out of place if you arrive in one. The guest list has been signed by such notables as Greta Garbo, André Kostelanetz, Salvador Dali, and Lily Pons. The Ingleside remains a very "in" place today, with an interesting contrast between the luxurious sedateness of the inn and the "swinging" atmosphere of Melvyn's Restaurant.

The Melvyn of the restaurant and inn is Melvyn Haber, the former manufacturer of all those cunning dogs with bobbing heads and plastic figurines that graced millions of autos in the past few decades. Melvyn took the fortune amassed from this business and spent several hundred thousand dollars renovating the old Ingleside. The original inn had been built as the Humphrey Birge estate during the 1920s by the heirs to the Pierce Arrow automobile fortune. Many of the original antiques that graced the Birge estate are found in the guest rooms at the inn, which are grandly large with oversize beds, stuffed armchairs, and large private bathrooms. Each room or villa contains its own steam bath and whirlpool, plus a refrigerator stocked with complimentary light snacks and beverages. The inn is particularly proud of its antiques, which include a bust of Petrarch's Laura, a vestment chest used by fifteenth-century priests, and a commode used by Mary Tudor. The inn's library contains leather chairs, backgammon sets, and a collection of the classics. On the grounds are a heated pool, shuffleboard, croquet, and miniature golf.

Dinner is served at the adjoining Melvyn's Restaurant in a setting dominated by wicker, bentwood, and white linen. The menu features American cooking with French Continental influence. Among the eight appetizers are shrimp or crabmeat cocktail, hearts of palm, pâté, and sliced salmon. The four soups available daily include a cold avocado and are followed by a choice of twenty-eight entrées such as chicken with tarragon, rack of lamb, tournedos of beef with shrimp and béarnaise sauce, steak Oscar, broiled salmon, lobster thermidor, scallops in Pernod. Entrée prices range from $9.95 to $16.95, and a complete dinner for two should average $40 to $50 plus the cost of wine. *Room Rates:* Rooms for two range from $75 to $330 per night. *Children and Pets:* Not permitted. *Driving Instructions:* From Los Angeles, take Freeway 10 into Palm Springs on Palm Canyon Drive. Continue about ¾ mile to Ramon Road, turn right and proceed one block to the entrance on the corner of Ramon and Belardo.

Rancho Santa Fe, California

Rancho Santa Fe has developed from land that was originally part of an 8,000-acre grant given to one Juan Osuna in 1845. In 1906, the Santa Fe Railroad purchased the grant for a mere $12 an acre from Osuna's heirs and began to experiment with raising eucalyptus trees for railroad ties. The land was carefully planted with 3 million seedlings, which soon grew into the impressive grove that survives today. But the wood proved unsuitable for use by the railroad, which then converted the remaining unplanted acreage into a citrus grove. A portion of the land was developed into a low-population density planned community, one of the first such communities in the country. Rancho Santa Fe is primarily residential. It is within one hour's drive of Mexico, the *Mount Palomar Observatory*, the *Scripp's Institute of Oceanography* at La Jolla, *Sea World* at Mission Bay, the *Wild Animal Park*, and the *San Diego Zoo* (as well as the many other attractions of San Diego).

THE INN AT RANCHO SANTA FE

Box 869, Rancho Santa Fe, CA 92067. 714-756-1131. *Innkeeper:* Dan Royce. Open all year.

The first building at the Inn at Rancho Santa Fe was the guest house, now part of the main building. The guest house was constructed by the Santa Fe Railroad as housing for prospective buyers of residential property in its surrounding planned community. The building was constructed of adobe that was dug from the building site. The inn property was purchased in 1941 by George Richardson, who, over the next fifteen years, developed the site into a country resort consisting of the original guest house and a variety of cottages, gardens, and walkways. In 1958, the inn was sold to the Royce family, which now in its third generation of hotel management, continues to operate the resort inn today.

The inn complex currently consists of seventy-five guest rooms in fifteen cottages as well as the original inn. All but one of the cottages are one story high, and each cottage guest room has separate air conditioning, a private sun terrace, and twin beds. Many of the cottage rooms and one suite in the main building have fireplaces, and some have kitchenettes. This is a full-service resort that is able to maintain its inn ambience through its landscaping and the attention of the staff. The main building has rough stucco walls, tiled and carpeted floors, high ceilings, and family antiques in its public rooms. The lounge frequently has a fire in the fireplace, and its walls are hung with old ship models. Recreational facilities at the inn include a heated swimming pool, three tennis courts, shuffleboard, badminton, table tennis, horseshoe pitching, and bowling on the green. Ocean swimming in the warmer months is available a few miles away at Del Mar beach, where beach cottages are available through the desk at the inn. There are several local golf courses that provide golf privileges to guests at Rancho Santa Fe.

The Inn's two dining rooms offer an à la carte menu that features steaks, seafood, poultry, and chops. In addition, there are three complete daily dinners that include soup or salad, potatoes, a vegetable, and rolls. Most of the soups, which include seafood chowders, lobster bisque, vichysoisse, cream of avocado, and French onion, among others, are homemade. The three entrées might include a nightly seafood dish such as poached or broiled salmon, egg-dipped abalone amandine, chicken cordon bleu or sautéed with wine and mushrooms, roast lamb, or a steak dish. Prices for the three evening specials generally range from $8.75 to $9.75, with steak dinners and several items on the à la carte menu bringing higher prices. *Room Rates:* Rooms in the main inn range from $26 to $52, with the Rose Garden fireplace suite going for $85. Cottage rooms range from $26 to $125 for a complete cottage apartment with kitchen, sitting room, two baths, bedroom, and fireplace. *Driving Instructions:* The inn is about 25 miles north of San Diego. Take I-5 to Lomas Santa Fe Drive and head inland for 5 miles.

Riverside, California

Riverside is a city of 140,000 about 50 miles east of the Pacific Coast in the Los Angeles area. Among the most popular tourist attractions in the area is the Mission Inn, a discussion of which follows. Besides catering to its own guests, the inn is open for tours. At the inn is a cross that was formerly installed at *Mount Rubidoux Memorial Park.* Formerly an important place for sun worship, the park, including the World Peace Tower, is open the year round from 9 A.M. to around dusk. Other popular tourist attractions in town are the *Orange Empire Railway Museum* at 2201 South A Street, the *Riverside Municipal Museum* (local history) at 3720 Orange Street, near the Mission Inn, and the *Sherman Indian Museum* at 9100 Magnolia Avenue.

THE MISSION INN

   3649 Seventh Street, Riverside, CA 92501. 714-784-0300. *Innkeeper:* Foster Davidoff. Open all year.

If you are within driving distance of Riverside, you must not miss the Mission Inn. Architecturally, it ranks as one of the twenty most unusual inns we know of in the United States. Beyond that it is a remarkable museum, filled with the riches of the four corners of the globe. To those uninitiated in the architecture of the West, the Mis-

sion Inn appears to be a careful restoration of an old California mission. In fact, the extraordinary building and its contents are results of the efforts of an energetic turn-of-the-century hotelier named Frank Miller.

An earlier hotel had existed on the site since 1876, but in 1902 Mr. Miller began his ambitious project of creating a modern hotel in the image of an early mission. The style of architecture known as Mission Revival dominates the main portion of the inn as it exists today. In time other wings were added, equally impressive. All have been restored to their elegance of 1935, the year Miller finished construction. The inn now contains numerous apartments, hotel rooms, function rooms, and a restaurant. It offers daily tours of its public rooms, definitely worth the time even if you are not a guest. One of the more important stops is the Cloister Music Room with its cathedral organ, stained-glass windows, heavy beams modeled after the San Miguel Mission, oak and mahogany parquet floors, and carved stalls in the style of Westminster Abbey. Presiding over the room are the stuffed remains of "Joseph," the popular macaw who was an inn resident from 1900 to 1939. The Spanish Art Gallery has carved doors from Spain, a seventeenth-century carved wooden candelabra, and stained-glass windows. The Signature Room has an overhead lighting fixture made of shells from the Philippines, and portions of the ceiling are from the twelfth century. This room contains some of the seven hundred bells the Millers had collected, plus Mr. Miller's collection of crosses. The adjoining Saint Cecilia Chapel has a rare signed Tiffany window portraying a monk at the organ. In the Atrio is a bronze copy of the Bacchus fountain of Prato, Italy. And so the tour continues through room after room, chapel after chapel. There are giant archways, elaborate plaster ornamentation, carved mahogany, and even catacombs below ground.

The guest rooms are equally impressive. Fifteen are available on a daily basis (plus a number of apartments). All have private bath. Each contains lovely antique pieces from the Millers' collection, and many have fireplaces. The rooms are sufficiently separated from the public rooms open to public tours so that guests' privacy is maintained.

The restaurant serves all three meals to guests and public. The dinner menu in the Spanish Dining Room is essentially the standard American menu (prime ribs, steaks, veal, duckling, etc.) with a slight international character. A *carne asada enchilada* combination includes steak sautéed in a spicy salsa plus an enchilada and flour tortillas. One or two dishes show some Italian overtones, such as the chicken Sicilian style. In general, entrées range from $6.50 to $10.95, with all other courses à la carte. *Room Rates:* Rooms range from $25 to $32 except the bridal suite, which is $60. *Pets:* Not permitted. *Driving Instructions:* From Anaheim, go east on Route 91. Take the University Street off-ramp and go left on University to Lime Street. Take a left on Seventh Street to the Mission Inn.

St. Helena, California

St. Helena is a town of 3,000 north of San Francisco on Route 29, in the center of one of California's richest wine-growing areas. There are tours of seventy wineries within one hour's drive and a great many in St. Helena itself. Among the more famous wineries of St. Helena are Christian Brothers, Louis M. Martini, and Inglenook. In addition to visits to these giants, there are interesting tours at the smaller Hanns Kornell Champagne Cellars and the Beringer Vineyards. The *Bale Grist Mill*, built in 1846, is in the process of being restored. It is open to the public as part of a state park on the outskirts of town. The *Silverado Museum* contains many of the effects of Robert Louis Stevenson, including manuscripts. It is closed on Mondays and holidays.

CHALET BERNENSIS

225 St. Helena Highway, St. Helena, CA 94574. 707-963-4423. *Innkeepers:* Jack and Essie Doty. Open all year.

The Chalet Bernensis is a fine old Victorian home built in 1884 by John Thomann, who also built the Sutter Home Winery next door. The Sutter Home Winery is still functioning but is now separate from the inn's property. The Sutter family bought the home after the death of Mr. Thomann, and one of the Sutter daughters lived there until 1946. When the Dotys purchased the property they first opened an antique shop and gallery on the first floor. Determined to restore rather than renovate, they gradually completed plans to open the old Sutter Home as an inn. A year later the Chalet Bernensis opened its doors.

The inn's furnishings and decorations all contribute to a feeling of the Victorian period. Here you will find lace doilies and curtains, quilted spreads, elaborate brass beds, impressive old chairs, and well-chosen reproduction wallpapers. Even the bathrooms were restored with their original claw-foot tubs and pedestal sinks. Queen-size beds are a concession to modern comfort. Adjacent to the original house, an old water tower is well on its way to being reconstructed into four additional guest rooms, each with private bathroom and fireplace. The yard has picnic tables for the guests and an old-fashioned porch with porch bench and swing for summer relaxation.

Breakfast is the only meal served here and consists of homemade scones, muffins, breads, jams, and jellies, as well as coffee and tea. *Room Rates:* Rooms without bath are $37.50, and with bath $45. *Pets and Children:* Pets and children under fifteen are not permitted; the inn prefers nonsmokers. *Driving Instructions:* St. Helena is about 17 miles north of Napa on Route 29.

San Francisco, California

San Francisco is a major urban cultural center and as such has many more attractions than could be given appropriate discussion in the space available in this book. We recommend that visitors write in advance for area information to the San Francisco Convention and Visitors Bureau, Office of Visitor Services, 1390 Market Street, San Francisco, CA 94102.

THE BED AND BREAKFAST INN
Four Charlton Court, San Francisco, CA 94123. 415-921-9784. *Innkeepers:* Robert and Marily Kavanaugh. Open all year.

The Bed and Breakfast Inn is an exquisite English-style pension in the heart of San Francisco. Bob and Marily spent hundreds of hours carefully restoring the Victorian buildings, which now contain eight rooms for overnight guests with a touch of European service in the middle of a modern, bustling city. When the Kavanaughs opened their doors in 1976, they offered five rooms in their home on Charlton Court, an English-mews-style street. The success of the original inn enabled them to open an annex next door that now offers three additional rooms that are particularly luxurious and offer private bathrooms. One has a sunken double tub. Both of the buildings were built in the latter part of the ninettenth century and thus predate the disastrous earthquake·of 1906.

The atmosphere here is cozy. The guest rooms, while not over-large, are warm and inviting. Each greets new arrivals with fresh fruit and flowers, and there are books and magazines in abundance. Some of the rooms open onto a garden courtyard. In each the guest may snuggle into a sea of quilts and down pillows. The mews totally isolates the guest from city noises. The only formal meal served is a Continental breakfast featuring croissants, freshly baked coffee cake, and coffee or tea. Guests are welcome to have breakfast in bed on trays set with Wedgwood china, linen napkins, and fresh flowers. Flowers here are, in fact, the keynote and guests are welcome in the inviting garden. *Room Rates:* Rooms with shared baths range from $32 to $52 a night. The elegant rooms with private bath are as high as $94 a night. All rates include continental breakfast. *Pets and Children:* Not permitted. *Driving Instructions:* The inn is on Charlton Court, a small street between Union and Buchanan streets off Union.

THE MANSION HOTEL

2220 Sacramento Street, San Francisco, CA 94115. 415-929-9444. *Innkeeper:* Robert C. Pritikin. Open all year.

This is not an ordinary hotel. Sadie the macaw has just bitten a hunk out of the grand piano. A ten-year-old rides on the back of a life-size plaster pig while the family dines before a mural that stretches over several walls and bears the title *Pig-nic.* The innkeeper entertains the willing (and one supposes an occasional unwilling) on his musical saw, playing such old favorites as "Moonlight Sawnata" and "Sawdust."

The saga of the Mansion began years ago when Bob Pritikin

heard the old Mansion was for sale. The place was littered with sleeping hulks of some of San Francisco's hippies, but Pritikin saw past the debris and bought the place. He tossed the hippies out and stepped back to discover he was suddenly in possession of a hotel in the city's high-rent district. His inaugural ball, so to speak, came two weeks later, when he gave a book party for one of his clients. To get ready for the party he dashed about from antique shop to antique wholesaler buying truckloads of whimsy, mostly from the Victorian era. Pritikin was content to leave no corner empty; the hotel spills over with treasures both real and fanciful. Mannequins in gowns that grandmother must have worn greet you in the grand foyer, a beaded purse collection hangs on one wall, reclaimed from a former spouse. Hotel guests can partake of the fun at an evening magic show complete with a nightly guaranteed appearance of Claudia, the mansion hauntress, plus a resident talking skull. Bob Pritikin emerges from the wings to entertain one and all on his saw Wednesday through Saturday evenings at 7.

The Mansion is a grand old home built in 1884 by a Senator Chambers, who had amassed a fortune from a profitable mining business. He was sheriff for a while and is reported to have presided over the first double hanging in the state. His daughter Claudia is the ghost who is believed to haunt the Mansion. Behind the generous measure of fun at the Mansion is a first-class hotel that has truly fine, comfortable furnishings, mostly of the Victorian period. The paneling that graces many walls could scarcely be replaced at any price. Beds

in the sixteen guest rooms are equipped with thick patchwork quilts. Many of the beds are brass, and there are fresh flowers and a raft of unusual accessories in each room. Some of the murals on the walls portray several distinguished San Franciscans. The remainder run heavily to pigs and unicorns and other mythological creatures. Surely a dominant feature, they are all by San Francisco artist Wayne Quinn. Most of the guests share bathrooms, but the register, nevertheless, has begun to read like a "Who's Who" of the West Coast. The good nature of the place helps a person to be cheerful while walking down the hall with a towel on one arm. Those who have come to expect other amenities, such as television, a telephone in the room, or room service, must put these thoughts behind them.

A quiche dinner that includes bean salad, fresh fruit, bread sticks, coffee, and wine is really the only evening repast. But never fear—it is San Francisco, after all, and fine food abounds nearby. *Room Rates:* Singles are $29 to $100. Doubles are $43 to $100. *Driving Instructions:* The hotel is four blocks west of Van Ness on Sacramento. It is five blocks from the California Street cable car stop.

Santa Barbara, California

Santa Barbara is a city of 72,000 on the coast north of Los Angeles. It has miles of free public beaches, several tennis clubs and golf courses, riding stables, fishing in the surf or from charter boats, and all the other amenities of a highly developed, affluent California community. Among the more important attractions in the city are the *Santa Barbara County Courthouse*, a Spanish-Moorish palace with hand-painted ceilings, carved doors, and imported tiles; *El Cuartel*, part of the original royal fortress built in 1782; the *Historical Society Museum* with extensive exhibits from Santa Barbara's past; the *Museum of Art*, a particularly fine if small museum with wide-ranging Oriental and American art; and *Mission Santa Barbara*, often called the Queen of California Missions. The *Museum of Natural History* features exhibits on mammals, birds, fish, and other wildlife of the Pacific Coast and Channel Islands.

Children should enjoy *A Child's Estate* with its small zoo in a delightful garden setting. Included are elephants, jungle cats, monkeys, a prairie dog village, and exotic birds. There is also a sealarium and a "Wild West" playground. For further area information contact the Santa Barbara Conference and Visitors Bureau, 1301 Santa Barbara Street, P.O. Box 299, Santa Barbara, CA 93103. The telephone number is 805-965-3021.

HOTEL UPHAM

1404 De La Vina St., Santa Barbara, CA 93101. 805-962-0058.
Innkeepers: Fred and Gela Percal. Open all year.

Amasa Lyman Lincoln was a Boston banker who settled in the Santa Barbara area in 1870 and soon noted that the growing city lacked hotel accommodations. He decided to build a sturdy two-story clapboard hotel with the broad eaves and widow's walk characteristic of his home state. The redwood for the building was brought from Santa Cruz to Santa Barbara and floated ashore.

What survives today is a small, old-fashioned city hotel, largely unchanged from the days of its construction. To be sure, there have been modernizations in the form of electricity and plumbing, and the building has acquired additions, but somehow the feeling is that of a time generations back. Outside are gardens that stretch up to the doorsteps of several cottages that provide additional accommodations. Inside, the decorations create a feeling of the Victorian era, with some antiques and reproductions capturing an even earlier period. A card room is provided for guests who wish to bring setups and liquor, as liquor is not served at the hotel. The hotel currently has forty-five guest rooms of which thirty-eight have private bathrooms. The dining room at the Hotel Upham serves breakfast, lunch, and dinner to guests and the public. *Room Rates:* Double rooms range from $28 to $29. Two rooms with connecting bath are $26 to $34 per night, and king-size beds are $32. *Pets and Children:* Pets are not permitted, and children are not encouraged. *Driving Instructions:* De La Vina Street is two blocks west of State Street, in the center of Santa Barbara.

Santa Catalina Island

Catalina is a small resort island almost 30 miles southwest of Los Angeles in the blue Pacific. Its capital, Avalon, is nestled in a natural crescent sweep of harbor surrounded by rugged mountains and the canyon of the Catalina Conservancy. The island is about 8 miles wide and 22 miles long. The *Visitor's Information and Services Center* is on Pleasure Pier in the center of Avalon on Crescent Beach. Visitors can pick up brochures of island attractions and sports oppurtunities, of which there are many. Tickets to the island tours can be purchased here. There are glass-bottom boat tours, nighttime flying fish spotting trips, inland tours, and sightseeing cruises. *Wrigley Memorial and Botanical Garden* is at the head of the picturesque Avalon Canyon. Tram service from Avalon is available. Below the imposing memorial is a botanical garden with cactus, succulents, and unusual plants indigenous to Catalina. The gardens are a scenic walk from town (1.7 miles). The only charge is for the tram, 50¢.

Golf is available at the Visitor's Country Club. The area in and around Avalon offers endless recreational opportunities, such as swimming in crystal-clear waters, horseback riding, tennis, scuba diving, bicycle rentals, fishing from piers and boats, and hiking and exploring mountain trails. Permits for interior hiking must be obtained from the Conservancy at 206 Metropole Ave., Avalon. The *Catalina Museum* and *Catalina Art Association Gallery* are both open daily in summer and weekends only in the off season. They are both in Avalon.

To get to Santa Catalina Island by sea or air by public transportation, reservations can be made with either the Catalina Air-Sea Terminal in San Pedro, near the south end of Harbor Freeway 11, in Long Beach at the Long Beach/Catalina Cruises Terminal on Golden Shore Boulevard, or at the Long Beach Municipal Airport, off Lakewood Boulevard. In summer only, there is a boat from Newport Beach at the Balboa Pavilion on Balboa Drive.

ZANE GREY PUEBLO HOTEL

199 Chimes Tower Road, Avalon, CA. Mailing address: Box 216, Avalon, CA 90704. 213-510-0966. *Innkeeper:* Karen Holliday. Open all year.

Perched high on one of Santa Catalina's knolls is the Zane Grey Pueblo. The pueblo was built by the famous Western author in 1926 as his private home. He fashioned it after the Indian homes of his beloved deserts of America's Southwest. It was at this home that he spent his later years, writing and fishing until his death in 1939. A large dirt patio had separated Grey's home from his brother Romer's house. That area has been transformed into a large fresh-water pool with cantilevered patio overlooking the harbor and ocean beyond. The sprawling estate has had several owners over the years and is now a peaceful, secluded hotel. Workmen who remember the construction of the house report that goat's milk was added to the mortar for strength. During recent renovations on the white stucco building, workmen bemoaned the durability of the mortared walls.

The spacious combination living room–dining room is a splendid lounge for guests. It offers guests the only television in the hotel and the use of a grand piano. The room boasts a massive fireplace with an interesting log mantle, a hand-hewn plank door, and open-beam ceilings. The exposed beams are of solid teak brought here from Tahiti by Grey on his fishing boat the *Fisherman*.

The hotel has eighteen guest rooms arranged off a long hall. This hall divides the rooms with spectacular ocean and harbor views from those overlooking the island's rugged hills and mountains. All of the rooms have private baths, queen-size beds, and wall-to-wall carpeting. Some have stucco fireplaces topped by log mantles. Some of the mountain-view rooms are extra large and airy. All the rooms are furnished in a modern hotel-motel style and are pleasant and comfortable. Guests are served complimentary toast and coffee at the big oak table in the living room. Coffee is always available.

The pueblo is surrounded by beautiful scenery. From its hillside perch there is a sharp drop to the road below. The hillside is covered with scrubby plants, small palms, and tall pines. Several steep stairways lead down to the road, and it is a mere three blocks from here to the main street of Avalon, the island's town. The hotel provides transportation to and from town and will pick up and deliver guests at the Boat and Air Terminal. *Room Rates:* May through October rates range from $25 to $45 according to room size. In the off-season, November through April, rates are $18 to $30. *Pets:* Not permitted. *Driving Instructions:* The hotel is on Catalina Island and can be reached by air or boat. See **Santa Catalina Island.**

Sausalito, California

You can drive to this artists' colony just outside of San Francisco over the Golden Gate Bridge, a properly majestic way to leave one great city and arrive at a lovely seaside village. The Army Corps of Engineers has constructed here a huge 1.5-acre model of the San Francisco Bay area, which it uses for testing the effects of tides and currents along the shoreline and in the estuaries that feed the bay. This model is open for visitors on a self-guided tour basis and for groups on a guided tour basis. Groups should call before arriving. During 1979, the 11-acre complex surrounding the model will be undergoing some extensive construction as part of a plan to convert the facility to a major visitors' center serving the Bay area. For this reason, it is best to call 415-332-3870 for information about what facilities are open to visitors before arriving. A flea market is held every weekend during good weather. The annual *Sausalito Art Festival* takes place every Labor Day.

CASA MADRONA HOTEL

156 Bulkley Avenue, Sausalito, CA 94965. 415-332-0502. *Innkeeper:* John W. Mays. Open all year.

In 1885, a wealthy Vermont-born lumber baron named William G. Barrett purchased a picturesque hillside property in Sausalito and proceeded to build his dream home high above the village. The Italianate home was a monument to the Victorian era, with marble fireplaces, stained-glass windows, brass chandeliers, and elaborate wrought-iron grillwork. Although Sausalito was ravaged by a great fire in 1893, the mansion escaped untouched except for some damage to the gardens. The manor house was a private home until 1902, when it was converted to a guest house. In the first half of this century it was called both the Casa Madrona Hotel and the Gallagher Inn. According to rumor, it was for a time a bordello. The early 1950s saw the inn become something of a combination beerhall and boarding house serving the beat generation. It was salvaged from the brink of ruin by the Deschamps family, who installed fashionable antiques and accoutrements and gradually transformed the inn into a European-style pension. The Deschamps created an elegant first-floor restaurant called Le Vivoir, which attracted an even larger clientele. The heavy rains of 1973–74 threatened to close the inn, and only the intervention of John Mays saved it. Mays saw the tremendous potential of the business and bought the property, pledging to restore the hotel to its former Victorian splendor. The Deschamps family continues to manage Le Vivoir, while the transformed hotel above it gains fame under owner John Mays.

The charming Victorian hotel is distinguished on its exterior by a wide thrust deck that sits out in front of a wide porch, all offering spectacular views of the bay below. Each of the fourteen rooms is decorated by an interesting assortment of Victorian and other antiques. There are a king-size canopied brass bed, a velvet love seat, and an antique English desk in the Royal Room; white wicker furniture and shutters in the Wicker Room; an unusual mahogany fireplace in the Fireside Room; red velvet, lace, and gilded-mirror décor in the Barbary Coast room; and similar treats in the other nine rooms in the main hotel. In addition, the Gate House is a secluded, vine-covered cottage with its own living room and separate bedroom and bath. There are two additional casitas that each sleep four, sometimes rented on a nightly basis when they are not occupied by people spending a full vacation there. The inn, incidentally, is within easy walking distance of the ferry to San Francisco.

Le Vivoir downstairs is an excellent, highly respected French restaurant. The candlelit dining room is decorated with fresh flowers daily. The menu includes such appetizers as *escargots bourguignon*, pike quenelles in lobster sauce (also availabe as an entrée), fresh salmon, and scampi. There is a solid daily list of soups that includes lobster bisque, turtle soup, French onion, and cream of leek and potato soup, among others. The entrée selections are lengthy and varied. A number are prepared for two, including squab in sage sauce, duckling cerise, rack of lamb, filet mignon with sauce Périgeux, and *lapin à la Forestiere*. Entrées for one include a vegetable platter, beef en brochette, *coq au vin*, sweetbreads and veal with cream and mushrooms. Desserts tend to run to the spectacular: strawberries Romanoff, peach flambée, or cherries jubilee. The humbler desserts include rum custard and chocolate mousse. A dinner for two with appetizer or soup, entrée, and dessert should run to about $36 on the average, not including gratuities and beverages. Enjoy a quiet and leisurely dinner downstairs, and then have the pleasure of remembering that it is but a few steps to your comfortable room upstairs. *Room Rates:* $30 to 35 for rooms without bath, $45 to $55 for rooms with bath, and $60 to $65 for the cottages. *Pets:* Permitted in cottages only. *Driving Instructions:* From San Francisco, take Route 101 over the Golden Gate Bridge and use the first exit (Alexander Avenue) to downtown Sausalito. Turn left at the first traffic light (Princess Street) and bear to the right.

THE SAUSALITO HOTEL

16 El Portal, Sausalito, CA 94965. 415-332-4155. *Innkeeper:* Liz MacDonald. Open all year.

The Sausalito Hotel was built in 1900 in the ornate Mission Revival style so popular at the turn of the century. The two-story corner hotel has a series of second-floor bay windows that serve the fifteen guest rooms plus a particularly impressive corner round bay. The first floor of the hotel is devoted to shops; the guest rooms and small lobby occupy the second floor.

Each of the rooms is furnished with antiques of the Victorian period, is decorated with appropriate wallpapers and swagged curtains at the windows, and has a hanging Victorian-style ceiling lamp. The Queen Victoria room has two arm chairs set into the curved large bay mentioned above and a carved high-back Victorian bed and matching marble-top dresser. In the Marquis de Queensbury room, you can recline in splendor in one of the most elaborate beds that we have come across, rivaling the one in the Vallejo Room at the Sonoma Hotel. This bed was once occupied by General Ulysses S. Grant. The room has the added attraction of a curved brick corner fireplace.

The other thirteen guest rooms, while not on such a grand scale, all offer comfort and elegance befitting the period.

The hotel is adjacent to the San Francisco ferry and surrounded by the many shops, restaurants, and galleries of this popular seaside village. At one time, bootleggers sought refuge in the Sausalito Hotel, and it is believed that Baby Face Nelson hid out here for a short while as well. Times are quieter now. The only meal served is the continental breakfast, but there are many fine local restaurants, including Le Vivoir at the nearby Casa Madrona Inn. *Room Rates:* Rooms range from $30 up to $65 for the Marquis de Queensbury room. Breakfast and parking are included in the room rates. *Driving Instructions:* The hotel is in the heart of Sausalito, immediately adjacent to the San Francisco ferry.

The Sea Ranch, California

The Sea Ranch is a privately developed community north of Jenner and south of Gualala. For information on the area, see **Gualala, California.**

THE SEA RANCH LODGE

Highway 1, The Sea Ranch, CA. Mailing address: P.O. Box 44, The Sea Ranch, CA 95497. 707-785-2371. *Innkeeper:* Ron Fitzgerald. Open all year except Christmas Eve and Christmas.

The Sea Ranch Lodge is a strikingly modern (1968) lodge at the edge of the Pacific Coast. It is a fine example of California architecture that draws heavily on the use of wood both in exterior design and in the public and guest rooms. The lodge has a variety of levels, with windows spotted unexpectedly in the broad expanses of vertical-board siding. Within the lodge, the wooden walls are broken only occasionally by stone fireplaces, picture windows, and splashes of primary color. Guest rooms are furnished in top-quality modern furniture of the sort found in a good modern hotel. In keeping with the lodge's recent construction, each of the twenty guest rooms has private bathrooms. Eight rooms have working fireplaces.

Guests may sit in the cathedral-beamed dining room and watch whales migrating along the coastline. In the spring, the meadow between the lodge and the sea is a field of blossoms. The view can be enjoyed from the lounge, with its stone fireplace. Guests use the solarium that adjoins the lounge for morning coffee or evening cocktails. The dining room offers eight American-style entrées, ranging from a vegetarian mushroom stroganoff for $4.75 through poached ling cod for $6.75 to New York steak for $10.25, all of which include salad, bread, and a vegetable. A selection of side dishes is available at à la carte prices.

The Sea Ranch Lodge was built by Oceanic California, Inc., which developed Sea Ranch, a second-home community that serves, primarily, residents of the San Francisco Bay area. Guests at the lodge may use the facilities of the recreation center that is part of that community, 3 miles north of the lodge. These facilities include an outdoor heated pool, three saunas, and three tennis courts. *Room Rates:* Rooms range from $36 to $48, depending on size and season. *Pets:* Permitted downstairs only. *Driving Instructions:* The lodge is 29 miles north of Jenner on Route 1, the seacoast highway.

Sonoma, California

Sonoma is in the heart of the Sonoma Valley wine country. The village was founded in 1835 as a distant outpost of the Mexican Empire, which had established its northernmost California mission there in 1823. After the Mexican hold on the area was relinquished to American control in 1847, the area gained fame when, in 1855, a Hungarian named Agoston Haraszthy settled in Sonoma and set out to re-create the winelands of his youth in Hungary. Having planted several hundred acres with the finest imported European rootstock, he built a stone winery in the Sonoma foothills, and the California wine industry was born.

Today, visitors are welcome to explore the *Mission San Francisco de Solano* on Spain Street and see the *Mexican Barracks* just across the street. The remains of *Casa Grande*, General Vallejo's home, which was largely destroyed by fire in 1867, are also on the same street. The *Blue Wing Inn* was built in 1840 by Vallejo and is across from the mission. *Buena Vista Winery*, 3 miles outside of town, was built in 1857 by Haraszthy and was the birthplace of the California wine industry. Tours and tasting are available there and in the *Hacienda Winery* nearby, also in the heart of the old Haraszthy vineyards. Numerous other Sonoma valley and Napa Valley vineyards are available for tasting and, in some cases, touring, all within an hour's drive. The *Jack London Home*, a beautiful stone house filled with London memorabilia, and the ruins of *Wolf House* are both in Glen Ellen, eight miles from Sonoma.

SONOMA HOTEL

110 West Spain Street, Sonoma, CA 95476. 707-996-2996. *Innkeepers:* John and Dorene Musilli (owners), and Mianna Haraszthy. Open all year.

In 1835, the Mexican authorities were alarmed: Russian settlers had made vast inroads on the Northern California coast, even going so far as to set up a fortress at Fort Ross, north of what is today Jenner. So Lieutenant Mariano Vallejo was dispatched northward to establish a military outpost in the area north of San Francisco and keep an eye on these strangers from the north. A logical spot for such an outpost, it seemed to Vallejo, was at the beautiful Mission San Francisco de Solano in the area now called Sonoma. Settling in quickly, he built adobe barracks for his soldiers, laid out a plaza, and built a home for himself and his family. Needing a name for his new pueblo, he chose "Sonoma," the Miwok Indian word for "valley of the moon." There

he remained for fifteen years, until he was displaced by a group of Americans who raised the Bear Flag on the Sonoma Plaza to inform Vallejo that California was now an American republic, a statement that became reality shortly after the conclusion of the Mexican War.

Today you can sleep in the bed previously owned by Vallejo's sister. This enormous carved-rosewood masterpiece rises to within inches of the wainscoted ceiling in Room 3, the Vallejo Room. The bed and its accompanying matched furniture are on loan from the Sonoma League of Historic Preservation. This bedroom and sixteen other handsome rooms, each beautifully decorated with impressive selections of matching and complementing antique furniture, all go to make up the singularly pleasing Sonoma Hotel.

Built in the 1870s, the hotel has had a varied and colorful history. It has housed a bar, a mercantile hall, a meeting hall, a boarding house, and, for a time, the Plaza Hotel, operated by the Sebastiani wine family. The present owners purchased the hotel and set about the monumental task of restoring it to a glory that certainly exceeds that of its predecessors. Layer after layer of paint was stripped away, wallpapers carefully chosen, luxurious curtaining selected, and etched-glass doors custom made. Do not despair if Room 3 is already booked. Room after room of almost equally exciting antiquity await your reservation. Take, for example, Room 1, which sports the most impressive brass bed that we have laid eyes on, Room 4 with its armoire of inlaid parquet, Room 2 with a five-piece matching suite with hand-carved designs topped by rare orange marble, or Room 6 with its solid oak bedroom set inlaid with ebony and an antechamber with a brass bed suitable for a third guest or child. Third-floor rooms run to the smaller sizes and are somewhat lower in price but have many choice antiques and should not be avoided. All the furnishings, the Musillis hasten to make clear, are authentic and came from private homes, auctions, antique stores, or antique shows. The chandeliers are authentic to the period, although many were brought to the hotel from the Midwest. The only meal served here is a continental breakfast. *Room Rates:* $28 for third-floor rooms with shared bath, $35 for second-floor rooms with outside bath, $40 for second-floor rooms with private bath, $45 for the Vallejo Room. *Pets:* Not permitted. *Children:* Not encouraged. *Driving instructions:* Sonoma is on Route 12 about 46 miles northeast of San Francisco.

Sonora, California

Sonora is a small town near the Columbia State Historical Park on Route 49. The town has a museum housed in the old County Jail that includes exhibits and tours of the old cells. However, tourists are warned that the museum will probably close for renovations during 1979. The Chamber of Commerce at 158 West Bradford Street in Sonora provides maps of the village that include a self-guided tour of about a dozen Victorian homes that have survived in the community. None may be entered, being private residences, but their history is outlined on the map. For other area information, see **Columbia, California.**

THE GUNN HOUSE MOTEL

286 South Washington Street, Sonora, CA 95370. 209-532-3421.
Innkeeper: Peggy Schoell. Open all year.
Hidden in the inner recesses of the Gunn House is Dr. Lewis Gunn's original two-story adobe. The highly opinionated liberal doctor came to the mother lode in the rush of 1849 and, in 1851, with the help of Mexican laborers, built the town's first adobe house. His family sailed around the Horn to join him in the colorful mining town. Dr. Gunn stirred a great deal of controversy with his newspaper, the *Sonora Herald*, the first in the area. His editorials were often quite unpopular with the rowdy miners and townspeople. At one point the

townspeople burned his presses in front of his house. The town of Sonora has become quite civilized since that time. Today it is a modern, bustling town of 3,000.

The Gunn House has undergone a great many changes and additions since its beginnings as a tiny home and office. Many porches and verandas were added, and several wings are stacked behind the old hotel on the very steep hillside. These buildings encircle a center courtyard of native stone patios and walls. There are rocking chairs and lounges around an oval heated pool. The inn's living room opens onto this sunken courtyard, as do many of the guest rooms. Margaret Dienelt, its present owner, rescued the Gunn House from destruction in the early 1960s. She spent years restoring the old building and making additions. The rooms throughout the hotel are impeccably and tastefully furnished with antiques of the Gold Rush era. Everywhere one looks there are marvelous converted oil lamps, ornate Victorian mirrors, marble-top dressers and tables, and a great variety of period couches, chairs, and bedsteads. The twenty-eight guest rooms have antique furnishings, shuttered windows, and quilted bedspreads. Most have private baths. Many of the rooms open onto the verandas. The rooms are equipped with unobtrusive television sets, phones, electric heat, and air-conditioning. In the warm months guests can relax and visit around the heated pool on the patio. On chilly evenings the big stone fireplace in the comfortable living room has a roaring blaze. The Gunn House does not serve food, but innkeeper Peggy Schoell will be glad to suggest places nearby. *Room Rates:* From $20.15 to $32.90, tax included. *Pets:* Small pets are permitted. *Driving Instructions:* Gunn House is in the heart of town. Sonora is on Route 108 at the edge of the Stanislaus National Forest.

Sutter Creek, California

Sutter Creek is resplendent with earth-tone accents, enhancing the restored period buildings that line its streets. It is a Western set that has survived the decades since the gold strikes. Today the town has a number of pleasant shops and offers visitors a chance to see the gradual evolution of Western building styles from the Gold Rush days into the early half of this century.

Knight's Foundry is the only water-driven foundry left in the country. The remains of many old gold mines survive in the area around the village. There are a number of antique and gift shops in town. Nearby Jackson is the home of the *Amador County Museum*, which houses an extensive collection of artifacts from the gold-mining period. Up the road to Pine Grove is *Indian Grinding Rock State Historic Park*, the remains of a Miwok Indian village, preserved by the state park system.

NINE EUREKA STREET

P.O. Box 386, Sutter Creek, CA 95685. 209-267-0342. *Innkeeper:* Helen Messick. Open all year except for occasional one-week vacations. Call ahead.

Tobias Lagomarsino and his family were early pioneers in the Sutter Creek area. The family had first come there in 1856, and they finally decided to build a suitable house in 1916. It still stands today at 9 Eureka Street, now an inn run by Helen Messick, who previously ran a similar place in the more hectic Carmel area. Mrs. Messick has kept her place purposely small.

The tidy house with broad front porch and single central dormer has only five guest rooms. By keeping the operation small, Mrs. Messick is able to devote her energy to the comfort of her guests. Each of the five bedrooms reflects her enthusiasm for a mixture on styles of antiques. The beds are completely individualistic—here one of those large high-backed Victorian numbers, there a pair of iron beds painted white, and elsewhere a pair of iron twins with spun-brass finials. Still another room has a sleigh bed poking out into the dormer area. All five rooms have private baths. The public rooms have a homey look accentuated by leather-covered stuffed furniture, wall-to-wall carpeting, and beamed ceilings. The front porch has a cozy corner filled with chairs, a wicker chest, potted plants, and the obligatory rocker. Breakfast here is a simple affair with fruit cup and homemade muffins or coffee cake the rule. It is the only meal served. *Room Rates:* $21 per room, the year round. *Pets and Children:* Not permitted. *Driving Instructions:* Sutter Creek may be reached by either Route 16 or Route 88.

SUTTER CREEK INN

75 Main Street, Sutter Creek, CA 95685. 209-267-5606. *Innkeeper:* Jane Way. Open all year except January.

Settled comfortably in the middle of this lovely gold-country town is the Sutter Creek Inn. As former New Englanders, it is easy for us to see what tugged at Jane Way's heartstrings when she first saw the handsome Greek Revival building with its distinct New England lines. One must presume that the look was chosen to placate the owner's bride, who had been transplanted from her native New Hampshire. When Jane first saw the place, in the mid-1960s, it was empty and looked a bit forlorn. It is hardly that now. It is crisply painted with its clapboard gleaming and its doors and shutters in pleasant contrasting tones. Inside, the main house has a large living room with a brick fireplace and a breakfast room with two big harvest tables for Jane's daily morning repast, the only meal served, but a full American-style meal it is.

The rooms vary in size. Some are in the main inn and some are out back in the former outbuildings, recently converted to particularly fine overnight accommodations. The choice of rooms is considerable, and the prices vary accordingly. Many of the rooms have beds that hang suspended from the ceilings by chains. These swinging beds have become Jane's trademark and are much sought after by many of her guests. Many rooms have fireplaces with a small supply of firewood provided. If more is needed, Jane recommends that you bring some from home or purchase it at one of the local grocery stores. The names of the rooms are, in some cases, more prosaic than their careful and attractive decorations. Thus you may stay in Tool Shed, Miner's Cabin, or Lower Washhouse. Definitely not prosaic is the Carriage House with a fireplace, queen-size bed,

and two bathrooms. It is the most expensive room in the house. *Room Rates:* Most rooms range from $28 to $32 on weekdays and $40 to $42 on weekends. The Carriage House is $55 and $65, respectively. There are a few smaller rooms available for $24. All rooms but the Carriage House require a two-day minimum stay on weekends. *Pets, Cigars, and Children:* Pets, cigars, and children under 15 are not permitted. *Driving Instructions:* The inn is 5 miles north of Jackson on Route 49.

Volcano, California

Volcano, like so many other mining towns, had a population that approached 10,000 in the 1860s. However, unlike many of its sister towns, it survived with some grace the decline that followed the exhaustion of the gold lodes. Many of the older buildings remain, although fire here, as elsewhere, took its toll. The town, partly because of its relative isolation from the traffic of Route 49, several miles distant, has no neon signs, ultramodern motels, gas stations, or supermarkets. It is an area rich in wildlife and a peaceful side trip for those exploring gold country. There is a fine swimming hole in nearby Sutter Creek. Local spots of interest include the *Indian Grinding Rock State Historical Park* on the road to Jackson and the

Jackson County Museum in Jackson. A county fair is held the second week of August in nearby Plymouth.

SAINT GEORGE HOTEL

2 Main Street, Volcano, CA Mailing address: P.O. Box 275, Volcano, CA 95689. 209-296-4458. *Innkeepers:* Marline and Charles Inman. Open all year except on Mondays and Tuesdays and for the first six weeks of the year.

The St. George Hotel is a humble three-story structure that managed to survive the rise and fall of this relatively well-preserved mining town. Two other hotels had flourished, if briefly, on this same spot in the mid-nineteenth century, but the Eureka and the Imperial both succumbed to the most common disaster of the era—uncontrolled fire. The St. George was constructed by its founder, B. F. George. Today, bedrooms are available on the two upper floors of the vine-covered, balconied building.

The rooms in the old hotel are mostly furnished with antiques. There is a lounge with a fireplace and an Old West bar that houses artifacts and pictures from the mining days. Rooms in the main hotel maintain the custom of the Gold Rush days of sharing a bath at the end of the hall on each floor. Hotel beds all have hand-crocheted bedspreads. There is a more modern annex built in 1961 that contains rooms with private bathrooms.

Dinners served nightly feature a single entrée, frequently prime ribs of beef or chicken. Soups, breads, and desserts that accompany the meal are all made in the hotel kitchen. This is a quiet and un-pretentious place in a town that has been largely untouched by the march of time. One can sit on the porch at twilight on an old bench, much as the miners did years ago, and hear the cry of a coyote from behind the limestone ruins of the old Wells Fargo office. It's not fancy, but it surely is peaceful. *Room Rates:* Rooms are available from $18.50, EP, or, double occupancy, $25 per person, MAP. *Pets and Children:* Permitted in annex rooms only. *Driving Instructions:* Drive east on Highway 88 to Pine Grove, then north on Volcano–Pine Grove Road to Volcano.

Westport, California (see Mendocino County)

COBWEB PALACE

Seaview and Highway 1, Westport, CA 95488. 707-964-5588.
Innkeeper: Doyle Dorsey. Open all year.

Back in the late nineteenth century, Westport was the largest of the
seaports between San Francisco and Eureka, from which the big
schooners carried off fortunes in timber harvested by the enormous
lumber companies of the redwood empire. The town at that time
had a population of 10,000 and supported seventeen saloons and
fourteen hotels. Today only one hotel still stands in the tiny town,
whose population has dwindled to 80. Cobweb Palace is an old Vic-
torian-Western hotel comprising a grouping of traditional "old West"
wood-fronted buildings—the old hotel and its restaurant, saloon, and
gift shop—all joined by a clattery old boardwalk covered by their
assorted porches and balconies. Nasturtiums, calla lilies, and ivies
grow in colorful profusion alongside the boardwalk and buildings and
even in the meadows beyond. The Cobweb Palace Hotel, with its
big, square "Western movie" front, sports a second-floor balcony
that is just perfect for whale-watching, the number-one pastime here.
Across the road (the famous scenic Coast Highway 1) is a peaceful
meadow where cows and horses graze and wildflowers bloom. Some
300 feet beyond is a 40-foot drop to the private little sandy beaches
carved out of the rugged rocks by the relentless sea; lovely paths
lead down to the shore where devoted lovers of seclusion can easily
find a cove all to themselves.

One of the nicest features of Cobweb Palace is its innkeeper-
owner, Doyle Dorsey. Hotels and inns tend to reflect their owners'

personalities, and this is certainly true of the Palace. The atmosphere here is friendly and charming and, while there is plenty of personal attention, things move at a quiet country pace.

The six guest rooms are furnished individually with a blend of period Western Victoriana, old wallpapers, and comfortable queen-size beds. Each room has its own private bath. The views from the windows are spectacular: Some look out over the Pacific and the rugged coast, and others offer vistas of the beautiful hills behind the hotel. The nearby surf lulls guests to sleep and wakens them in the morning, and no jarring sounds of television or radio break the spell.

Downstairs, the lobby is a cozy lounge where guests can sit on a rainy, cool evening and enjoy the warmth of the old parlor stove. While there are plenty of books, newspapers, and cards to amuse folks, the favorite activity seems to be lively conversation. The next room is a combination dining room and old-fashioned saloon. The candlelit dining room overlooks the meadows and ocean. The Victorian oak tables are covered with crisp white tablecloths and napkins. The menu features fresh seafood brought in by local fishermen and clammers. For the "beef or nothing" crowd, there are a variety of steaks and chops also. Meals come complete with a homemade soup, garden-fresh salad, the main entrée, dessert, and coffee for about $7.50 to $8.50. Both the saloon and the dining room offer a large selection of wines in addition to the usual liquors and beers. Weekends, the restaurant is open to guests and the public. Sundays, brunch is served from 10 A.M. to 1 P.M.

Cobweb Palace is quite remote; the sea is its front yard; the mountains, the backyard; and all around the tiny Victorian town of Westport are miles of virtually untouched wilderness. The nearest neighboring town is 15 miles away. Visitors can hike and explore about in the hills and along secluded beaches, watch the passing parade of whales and dolphins, or just plain relax. *Room Rates:* Rates are $25 to $30 for a double room. *Driving Instructions:* Drive north on Coast Highway 1 from Fort Bragg.

DEHAVEN VALLEY FARM

P.O. Box 128, Westport, CA 95488. 707-964-2931. *Innkeepers:* Ronald D. Albrecht and Harry Cowan. Open all year.
Dehaven Valley Farm was built in the 1860s on a hillside overlooking

both the dramatic Mendocino County coast and the pine forests on the western slopes of the Dehaven Valley. The Victorian farmhouse is surrounded by lawns, flowers, and herbs whose many scents perfume the clear sea air. A grove of trees form a canopy over the Dehaven Creek as it flows past the farm and on to the nearby Pacific. Its water is clean, clear, and drinkable all year. There are acres of fields, hills, and pine forests for guests to explore. Old lumbering tools and farm implements are half hidden in rambling black-berry bushes that have sprung up in the fields around the farm. In addition to the farm animals here all sorts of wild birds can be observed, such as white herons, owls, quail, hawks, geese, and ducks. Their calls add excitment to the peaceful sounds of the valley. Guests have the extra privilege of watching whales, porpoises, and sea otters as they swim by this coastal farm.

The interior of the house is as charming as the exterior. The five upstairs guest rooms have individual personalities, with color as their main motif. The Red Room has an antique brass bed with burgundy crocheted bedspread, a china pitcher and basin, antique furnishings, and a delicate floral wallpaper. The Yellow, Turquoise, and Green Rooms have double beds and equally attractive furnishings. The Blue Room has twin beds. The rooms share a natural-wood upstairs bathroom containing an antique oversize bathtub. Downstairs, through the high-ceilinged living room with its fireplace, chiming antique clock, and well-stocked library, is the White Room in a quiet corner of the old house. It has a hall bath with full tub and shower. Above the kitchen is a special room named the Dehaven Suite, formerly the farm's master bedroom. The room has a high-beamed cathedral ceiling and huge picture window overlooking the valley and green hills. It has its own fireplace, bath, king-size bed, and private entrace.

The new owners, Ron Albrecht and Harry Cowan, are in the process of turning the 40-acre property into a self-sufficient working farm. They serve a great deal of their own produce at the inn, free from the processing and additives so often found in today's ingredients. The superb meals (breakfast and dinner) are served to public and guests in the bright, attractive dining room with its round oak tables and heirloom chairs. The kitchen is just off the dining room, and guests can smell and hear the makings of the six-course country dinner. Every meal is a unique creation depending on seasonal items from the farm and nearby fishing villages. All meals are accompanied by local red and white wines, fresh green salads, and a fruit and cheese plate. A dinner might begin with snails in mushroom caps, seafood crepes with garlic butter, or an artichoke with homemade mayonnaise. Soup could be a leek and watercress marvel, a fresh tomato soup, or possibly a tart cream of sorrel. Main courses include fresh ling cod à la Vera Cruz with rice and green beans; leg of lamb with garlic and rosemary served with dolmas and tomatoes provençal; and Cornish game hens with chestnut dressing and a side of fresh broccoli with lemon butter. The desserts come with plenty of steaming hot coffee or tea.

Dehaven Valley Farm brings back memories of childhood summers, visits to the grandparents, and the peaceful solitude of years gone by. The mood is serene and made for travelers wishing for clear water, fresh air, and a place to relax. *Room Rates:* $35 per room double occupancy, including continental breakfast for two. Dehaven Suite is $50 with breakfast for two. *Children and Pets:* Not permitted. *Driving Instructions:* From Westport, drive north on Route 1 for 2½ miles. The first dirt road after Branscomb Road is the entrance to the farm. Westport is north of Mendocino and Fort Bragg on the coast highway, Route 1.

Yosemite, California

Yosemite is much more than just the valley, and it certainly is much more than just a summertime experience. However, it is in the valley in the summer that most tourists begin to explore the park. Traffic jams and crowding have recently been ameliorated somewhat, owing to the park's tighter new regulations concerning traffic in the valley and the instituting of a valley-wide tram-bus mass-transit system. Some of the park's most famous sights, *El Capitan* (the world's largest granite monolith), *Half Dome, Yosemite Falls*, and *Bridalveil Falls*, are in the valley.

Outside the valley, visitors are urged to visit *Tuolumne Meadows*, an alpine gardenland with sparkling streams, glistening lakes, and mountain flowers all at an elevation of about 8,600 feet. *Glacier Point* offers a breathtaking vista overlooking the High Sierras, including a profile view of the famous Half Dome. To see the sequoias at their finest, stop at *Mariposa Grove* in the southern part of the park. Some of the giant trees reach 96 feet in circumference and up to 234 feet in height. The historical exhibits at the *Pioneer Yosemite History Center* in Wawona are of interest to all family members, as is the *Indian Cultural Museum* at park headquarters in Yosemite Village.

Yosemite has been a skiing center since the mid-1930s. It has a well-developed downhill skiing program at *Badger Pass* with twelve runs and trails and a GLM ski school. Cross-country skiing is taught in several full-day programs, including ones on touring survival and overnight ski-camping trips. Whatever season you visit Yosemite, it is important to remember not to be trapped into staying only in the valley. There are 1,200 square miles of wilderness at the park, hence little excuse for complaining about overcrowding.

AHWAHNEE HOTEL

Yosemite National Park, CA 95389. 209-373-4171. *Innkeeper*: John O'Neill. Open all year except from just after Thanksgiving weekend until Christmas vacation.

During the mid-1920s the then director of the National Park Service, Stephen T. Mather, had been embarrassed when a member of English nobility had refused to stay at the old Sentinal Hotel on the park grounds. He then ordered the two rival concession companies on the grounds to stop bickering with each other and join

forces to construct a luxury hotel. The Ahwahnee, the product of that rapprochement, in the final reckoning cost $1 million to build plus $250,000 for interior decoration. A serious effort was made to soundproof the building so that the roar of Yosemite Falls would not disturb light sleepers. Ultimately, defeat was admitted in trying to keep the water's song out of the hotel. Today, as in 1927, it is the sound of Yosemite's greatest falls that lulls guests to sleep.

The grandeur of the building is evident as soon as you enter the lobby. Tall picture windows overlook the magnificent scenes of Yosemite Valley and seem to unite the spectacle of nature outside and the spectacle of artifacts within. The main dining room has huge sugar pine beams and exposed granite columns rising to a ceiling height of 34 feet. Other public rooms include the almost as impressive Great Lounge, the Solarium, Mural Room, Winter Club Room, Tudor Lounge, Under Lounge, and Colonial Room. During winter months, the Great Lounge fireplace sheds a warm glow in the evening. Tea is served there in the afternoon, and demitasses at night. Throughout the public rooms hang elaborate wrought-iron light fixtures and tapestries. The repeating Indian patterns that are a characteristic of the Ahwahnee are worked into the floors and walls.

The 121 guest rooms are also decorated with an Indian theme; colorful tiles are arranged in an Indian-type pattern in their private bathrooms. The hallways have Indian-style borders along the tops of the walls, and each guest room doorway is also done with an Indian pattern. The spacious grounds include a well-groomed lawn and natural areas that blend into the meadows and pine forests. There are two tennis courts, a pitch-and-putt golf course, and a heated swimming pool. In addition to the rooms in the main building, there are several cottages by the hotel.

As at the nearby Wawona Hotel, guests are expected to dress for dinner. In keeping with the elegance of the surroundings, the food is among the finest in the West and certainly worth a visit to the hotel for those who are staying elsewhere in the park. There are several choices of appetizer, including artichoke with mustard mayonnaise, Bismarck herring, smoked salmon, and *escargots bourguignon*. The hotel serves a variety of soups, from the more commonly encountered tomato or mushroom to cream of zucchini and cream of spinach. The soups are included with the price of the entrée which also includes relish tray, green salad, potato, vegetable, hot rolls and butter, and beverage. There are eleven entrées, including rainbow trout sauté amandine; filet of northern salmon; lobster thermidor; a variety of omelets; breast of chicken epicure; prime ribs of beef; roast duckling Montmercy; Chateaubriand, sauce Béarnaise; and loin lamb chops. Entrée prices range from $5.75 for the omelet to $11.50 for the lobster. The appetizers range from $1.50 to $3.50, and desserts hover around $1. Starting the second Thursday in January and running every Thursday through ski season, there is a skiers' buffet supper. The Ahwahnee buffet far surpasses the usual hastily assembled array of cold platters. *Room Rates*: The rates for the 121 rooms range from $40 for a parlor room to $50 for most doubles. Single rooms are $42. *Pets*: Not permitted. *Driving Instructions*: Take Route 120, 140, or 41 to Yosemite National Park; follow the signs to Yosemite Valley. At Yosemite Village, follow the signs to the Ahwahnee Hotel.

WAWONA HOTEL

Yosemite National Park, CA 95389. 209-373-4171. *Innkeeper*: Bob La Croix. Open April through November.

This fine old Victorian resort hotel got its start back in 1856, when Galen Clark homesteaded in the Wawona basin. Mr. Clark was suffering from tuberculosis and had been told that he had just a year or two left to live. He came to the mountains to die among the scenic wonders of Yosemite and proceeded to live for fifty-three more years, finally succumbing at the age of ninety-six.

The plot of land that Clark chose to develop when he came to Yosemite was a full day's ride from the stagecoach line's end. Thus he found himself playing host to many people forced to spend the night, and he was eventually prompted to build rooms to accommodate guests on a paying basis. Clark was not much of a businessman and was soon at the verge of going broke. He found a partner, Edwin Moore, and together they held the hotel business together, although marginally, until 1870, when they sold the property to the Washburn brothers. The Washburns brought the hotel complex into its own. They constructed what is now the main hotel building in 1879, another building in 1885, and the Annex in 1915. Finally, in 1934, they sold their land and hotel to the National Park Service. Since 1934 it has been run by the current owners, Yosemite Park and the Curry Company. The hotel is listed in the National Register of Historic Places.

This Victorian-era hotel has gingerbread eaves, a gleaming white exterior, and wide verandas that reflect the California heritage of Spanish haciendas. Hop vines decorate the building's front in the summer months. Towering incense cedar trees shade the lawn, and lawn chairs are scattered about much as they might have been fifty or more years ago. In fact, it is easy to imagine finely attired young Victorian women and their escorts strolling in the afternoon sun here.

The hotel's interior is furnished with antiques and decorated to conform to the atmosphere that prevailed in the late nineteenth century. The Sun Room, in the Annex, is a public lounge decorated with rattan furniture and exquisite inlaid wood paneling. In the dining room, the lamps, made in 1917, are decorated with hand-painted scenes of the giant sequoias in the nearby grove of big trees. Approximately half of the guest rooms have antique bedsteads, either wood or brass. Each room opens onto the veranda overlooking the broad lawns surrounding the buildings. Of the fifty-three guest rooms, the majority have private bathrooms.

The dining room at the Wawona is not on the grand scale of the Ahwahnee. But here, as well, guests are expected to dress for dinner. In today's terms, this means that jackets are required and ties preferred for men, and pants suits or dresses for women. The dinner menu at Wawona has five entrées nightly, consisting of grilled rainbow trout, Southern fried chicken, broiled chopped sirloin, prime ribs of beef, and omelets. Included are the relish tray, choice of juice or fruit cocktail, soup of the day, and the other dinner accompaniments. The Wawona's guests are welcome to take their meals at the Ahwahnee if they prefer. *Room Rates:* Two rooms with connecting bath for four people, $35. Rooms without bath are $14.50, and rooms with bath are $23.50 to $25.50. *Pets:* Not permitted. *Driving Instructions:* From Fresno, take Route 41 to Yosemite National Park; the hotel is set back from the road within the park. From other directions, after arriving in Yosemite, take Wawona Road to the hotel.

Yountville, California

Yountville is a town of about 2,300 an hour and a half north of San Francisco. The town is in the center of the Napa Valley, which has more than sixty wineries. Tours are available at most. They range in size from the giants of the area like Martini, Inglenook, and Mondavi down to some of the small, estate-type bottlers of premium wine such as Stony Hill, Chappellet, Freemark Abbey, and others. In addition to winery tours, a popular tourist stopping place is the *Robert Louis Stevenson Museum* in nearby St. Helena.

BURGUNDY HOUSE COUNTRY INN

6711 Washington Street, Yountville, CA 94599. 707-944-2711. *Innkeeper:* Mary Keenan. Open all year.

Situated in the heart of the wine country of Napa Valley, Burgundy House was built as a winery in the 1870s. Charles Rouvegneau and his workers set out to build a winery that would stand the test of time. They wrested native fieldstone from the surrounding countryside and put up 22-inch-thick walls around stout hand-hewn posts and beams. The result is a rough-stone two-and-a-half-story historic structure that is cool in the summer and cozy around the huge hearth when days turn crisp.

The rooms are furnished with the many antiques belonging to the innkeepers, who are former antique dealers. Surrounding the main inn are three cottages that sleep four each. These were fashioned from the old Justice Court, mayor's house, and livery stable.

In addition, the Keenans plan to construct a new inn on the property that will be completed some time in 1979 and will offer six guest rooms, all with private baths.

This inn, inspired by the wine industry that stretches for miles in every direction from its doorstep, provides its guests with complimentary wine, set out on the sideboard, and there are filled wine carafes in every guest room, compliments of the inn. Also included in the room rate is a continental breakfast of coffee, juice, tea, fruit, melon, berries, and an assortment of pastries. *Room Rates*: Single rooms are $35, double rooms and cottages are $45 per couple. *Pets and Children*: Permitted in cottages only. *Driving Instructions*: Take I-80 north from San Francisco to Route 29, and Route 29 north to Yountville.

MAGNOLIA HOTEL

6529 Yount Street, Yountville, CA. Mailing address: P.O. Drawer M, Yountville, CA 94599. 707-944-2056. *Innkeepers*: Bruce and Bonnie Locken. Open all year.

This hotel was built in 1873 of stones hauled from a nearby quarry. The adjoining restaurant was built in 1900 of bricks rescued from an old church that was being torn down in the village. Before that, the bricks had served as ballast for a ship that bore them from Europe. The stone walls are up to 28 inches thick, surely safe enough to brave even a latter-day earthquake.

In days gone by, the hotel served as a bordello, a working man's hotel, a 4-H headquarters, and the local center for rum-running during Prohibition. Today, it has been restored to a new level of comfort and it contains seven guest rooms, each with private bath. Many of the rooms have either exposed-brick or stone walls. The beds have brass or carved Victorian headboards and simple furnishings that include period lamps and floral wall-to-wall carpeting. A complimentary decanter of port graces a table in every guest room. On each bed is a special touch of Bonnie's—a handmade cloth doll unique to the room it lives in.

As you enter the hotel, you are greeted by the lobby, with its antique rolltop desk. Also on this floor is the dining room, used for breakfast service only. Guests may gather in the parlor on this floor, which is equipped with a baby grand piano. Farther back on the first floor are the hotel kitchen and one of the guest rooms. A redwood deck at the rear of the hotel contains the heated Jacuzzi 12-foot spa that is used all year. On the grounds is a heated pool.

The restaurant at the Magnolia is connected to the inn via its rough-stone wine cellar. Hotel guests enter the restaurant through a street-level entrance rather than from within the hotel. Once inside they are surrounded by the brick and stone walls of an intimate restaurant that is warm with the glow of a fire in the fireplace and contains tables set with white tablecloths over maroon velvet. A crystal candlestick graces each table. Stone steps lead to the wine cellar, currently stocked with more than three thousand bottles of more than two hundred California wines. This award-winning restaurant (1979 *Travel-Holiday* award) is completely under the direction of Bonnie Locken. She has purposely kept it small (seating thirty), and it serves in seatings that begin every fifteen minutes. In this way, guests can proceed unhurriedly through a meal that begins with the waitress explaining the day's menu. As a rule, for instance, Bonnie offers pork, lamb, or veal on Thursdays; fresh fish, lobster, or shrimp on Fridays; beef on Saturdays and poultry on Sundays. Part of her success has come from her uncompromising requirement that no frozen food be used and that all food be prepared by her and her staff on the premises. The only exception to the rule is the sourdough French bread, which is partially cooked expressly for the restaurant by a commercial bakery and finished at the hotel. *Room Rates*: Rooms range from $48 to $65 and include a full breakfast. *Pets and Children*: Not permitted. *Driving Instructions*: Yountville is located 9 miles north of Napa. Take the "Yountville-Veterans Home" exit off Highway 29.

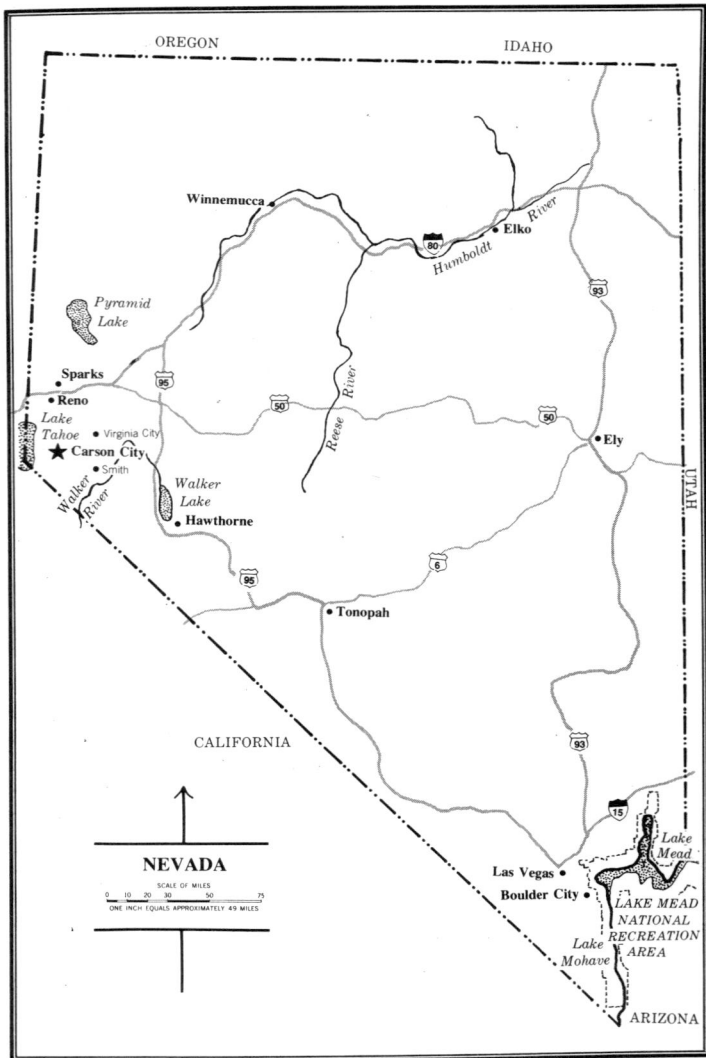

OREGON   IDAHO

Winnemucca

80   Elko   River

Humboldt

93

Pyramid
Lake

Sparks
95
Reno
Lake
Tahoe   50
Virginia City   Reese River   50   Ely
★ Carson City
Smith
Walker
River   Walker
Lake
Hawthorne

6

95

Tonopah

CALIFORNIA

93

15

NEVADA

SCALE OF MILES
0   10   20   30   50   75
ONE INCH EQUALS APPROXIMATELY 49 MILES

Las Vegas ●   Lake
Mead
Boulder City ●
LAKE MEAD
NATIONAL
RECREATION
AREA
Lake
Mohave

ARIZONA

UTAH

Nevada

NEVADA SHOWS EVIDENCE of having been populated by primitive tribes as early as 20,000 B.C. Compared to the neighboring states, however, Nevada was late in coming under exploration by the white man. Some early parties probably reached parts of Nevada in 1776, but active exploration did not occur until the period from 1825 to 1830. Trade with the regions of California, Arizona, and New Mexico was enhanced by the opening of the Santa Fe trail in 1830.

Nevada, like much of the Southwest, was given to the United States as part of the settlement of the Mexican War in 1848. The further development of Nevada followed soon after, as Mormon settlers led by Brigham Young arrived in the Utah-Nevada area. The Mormons never had a firm hold on the territory and withdrew to Salt Lake City after a few years. In 1859 Henry Comstock and other miners found silver in the area of what was soon to become Virginia City. Almost a billion dollars' worth of the precious mineral was removed from the Comstock and other mines in the next thirty years. President James Buchanan recognized the need for a loyal and wealthy Northern territory and created the Nevada Territory. Statehood was granted in 1864, and money from the silver mines helped to finance the Union troops.

By the 1890s, the silver mines had become exhausted and silver prices had dropped to the point where mines with low-grade ore could not continue to operate economically. Ranching became the main source of income in the state for many years, although there was a renaissance of mining in the early part of this century after the discovery of new mineral sources, primarily gold and copper. In the early twentieth century, the Nevada legislature passed laws providing for relatively easy divorces, and later, in 1931, laws were passed making gambling legal. Gambling is now a major source of income within the state, with casinos active in any city of size, especially Reno and Las Vegas. For travel information write to the State of Nevada Travel Division, Department of Economic Development, Carson City, NV 89710. The telephone number is 702-885-4322.

Gold Hill, Nevada (see Virginia City, Nevada)

GOLD HILL HOTEL AND TAVERN

218 Main Street, Gold Hill, NV. Mailing address: Box 304, Virginia City, NV 89440. 702-847-0111. *Innkeepers:* Dorothy and Fred Immoor. Open all year.

The Gold Hill Hotel is one of the oldest hotels in Nevada. As a sign on the porch states, "This is the first edifice known to Nevada to be worthy the name of hotel." Just half a mile from historic Virginia City, the hotel was built in 1859 on the first mining claim recorded for the Comstock Lode. The hotel was listed as "old" on an 1879 insurance map of the area. Some twenty years ago, Fred and Dorothy Immoor were visiting Virginia City as tourists, indulging in their favorite pastime—antiquing. Before they knew it, they had fallen in love with a giant antique—the Gold Hill Hotel. When they first encountered the building, it was a mess, hidden under layer after layer of "modern improvements." The Immoors stripped the walls, floors, and ceilings clean and uncovered the beautiful rough stone walls, brick floors, and hand-hewn woods. Now that the exterior has been cleaned up, the hotel looks ancient and austere. Its lines are classically simple and unmistakably Western. The stones and bricks used in the construction and renovation are worn and weather-beaten. A white balcony supported by turned white pillars stands out in vivid contrast against the gray of the stones and the muted orange of the bricks. The rocky hills form a stark backdrop to the place.

Entering the lobby, one is instantly catapulted into the rustic, colorful past of the Gold Rush. The room is chock full of period antiques from the West's earliest mining boom towns—Gold Hill, Virginia City, and Silver City—including the hotel's original cash register and a stone fireplace. The adjoining rooms house the old tavern, which has a restored wine cellar and the original bar where many famous and infamous characters used to bend an elbow.

Up the wooden staircase along the outside stone wall are the five guest rooms, each furnished with Victorian antiques from the area. The bridal suite has a four-poster bed with an antique white canopy and matching bedspread; a cozy red comforter is folded invitingly at its foot. All the bedrooms contain marble-top dressers, mirrors, washstands with pitchers and bowls, and antique brass beds. The guests share the old-fashioned stone-floored bathroom with its massive claw-foot tub.

In the evening, guests may join Dorothy and Fred in the tavern, where everyone cooks his own thick filet mignon in the red hot coals of the fireplace. The Immoors prepare the rest of the meal's fixings while guests supervise the steaks. Fresh green salads, bread hot from the wood-burning oven, and perhaps baked potatoes are heaped on the long table with its checkered cloth. The public also may dine here with advance reservations. *Room Rates*: Rooms are $18.50 a double. *Pets*: Not permitted. *Driving Instructions*: The hotel is in Gold Hill half a mile south of Virginia City on Route 17 between Routes 50 and 395.

Smith, Nevada

Smith is about 80 miles south of Reno, in Smith's Valley, a green valley in the Sierra Nevadas. Two tiny villages, Smith and Wellington, are the only settlements here, in an oasis of greenery in a state that is largely desert. The Bidwell Trail, once the route of the first migrants to cross the state in 1841, passes through the valley. In 1859, four settlers (two named Smith) made the incredible trek across the Sierra Nevadas and settled the valley. They had come from California in search of good pasture lands.

In the mountains on either side of the valley visitors will find fascinating canyons and ghost towns to explore. Ask in either town for suggestions and directions. The area is quite beautiful and relatively untouched. For skiers and visitors wanting to try their luck at the tables, Reno and Lake Tahoe are not far to the north. For other area suggestions, see **Virginia City, Nevada**.

WINDYBRUSH RANCH
Artist View, Smith, NV. Mailing address: Box 85, Smith, NV

89430. 702-465-2481. *Innkeepers*: Frank and Margaret Parsons. Open all year.

Windybrush Ranch is the place for a real getaway—far from civilization's cares and woes. It is no dude ranch, but the real article. The Parsonses offer two large Western guest rooms and a big family bunkroom in their ranch house. They so love their secluded peaceful life that they would like to share it with a few lucky guests. The ranch property was originally part of a homestead in the mid-nineteenth century. Smith's Valley is nestled between two big mountain ranges. Situated on the east side of the beautiful Sierras, the ranch offers views of the high, snow-capped peaks all year.

Windybrush is a small, self-sufficient ranch with a large vegetable garden and lots of small livestock, such as ducks, turkeys, chickens, goats, and sheep. It is surrounded by enormous ranches with their thousands of acres and thousands of sheep and cattle. The entire valley offers prospects of unlimited beauty and interest; coyotes howl at night, deer come and nibble in the garden, and wild birds of many sizes can be spotted. No hunting is permitted. In spring the desert flowers bloom profusely, and their scents mingle with the smell of the pines, sage, and garden flowers.

The Walker River flows nearby, within walking distance. The Parsonses will prepare any fish caught by a guest, if the fisherman cleans it first. Margaret and Frank will also pack a hearty picnic lunch for an exploratory jaunt to the nearby mountains or a neighboring ghost town. The Parsonses will bed down (or otherwise put up) anything from a goldfish to Old Dobbin as long as the owners do the caretaking. Meals at the ranch are served family style in the kitchen or dining room. Generous portions are served at all meals. All meals are included in the room rates, and there are always steaming hot coffee, tea, and snacking cookies available at any time. The Parsonses provide transportation to many area attractions, special attention to people on special diets, or just the peace and quiet of a beautiful clear night with billions of stars. Here is a chance to do absolutely nothing if that is what you want. To sit in a rocker on the front porch and listen to country sounds, smell the country air, see how blue the sky is, and "see some open space that has been almost the same from the time God created it." *Room Rates*: Adults, $16 a day or $96 a week. Children 6–12 are $9 a day or $55 a week. Children under six are free, all AP. Off season (October to April) is 10 percent less.

Driving Instructions: From Reno go south on Route 395, 66 miles to Route 3. Turn left, go 11 miles to Smith Valley. When you enter Smith Valley, go about three-quarters of a mile downhill and across the bridge, then turn left on Colony Road. Travel 5 miles to Artist View on the right. Go 4 miles on Artist View until you see the Windybrush Ranch sign off the road on the left.

Virginia City, Nevada

This historic old mining town is situated between Carson City and Reno on the far western edge of the state. Virginia City flourished as a mining town in the mid-nineteenth century. It was known as the Queen of the Comstock Lode, and its mines produced nearly a billion dollars in gold and silver, helping to finance the building of San Francisco and the Union Army in the Civil War. The town is a popular tourist attraction, visited by half a million people annually. The silver kings built themselves fabulous mansions and saloons; these marvels and the old mines, *Chinatown*, and the *Piper's Opera House* stood virtually untouched from the mines' closings in the early twentieth century through World War II. After the war the town began its comeback and is now a flourishing, elegant restoration town. Private owners have painstakingly restored the Victorian homes and mansions. The Piper's Opera House, the mansions, and saloons are open to visitors. There are mine tours, and in summer the *V & T Railroad* is a popular tourist ride. Virtually every building in this town is of historic significance. The town provides guided tours and visitor's maps of the area.

SAVAGE MANSION

146 South D Street, Virginia City, NV. Mailing address: P.O. Box 445, Virginia City, NV 89440. 702-847-0574. *Innkeepers*: Bob and Irene Kugler and Ann Louise Mertz. Open all year.

In 1879, former President Ulysses S. Grant came to Virginia City especially to thank the miners there for the millions of dollars of gold and silver that they had wrenched from the hillsides surrounding the city. Grant and his wife toured the mines and were feted in grand style, including an elaborate roast beef dinner at the Savage Mansion. They remained at the mansion for two nights in the room that is now

called the Grant Room, one of three available to overnight guests in this restored Victorian mansion. Even as Grant spoke, the grand old lady of a mining city was on the verge of plummeting into decline. Fire had destroyed vast portions of the town four years earlier, and the mines would no longer be as highly productive. In the ensuing years, time would take its toll on the Savage Mansion, and it would sink almost to ruin before being saved by the heroic restoration effort of the current owners.

The mansion was built in 1861 as the beautiful home of the superintendent of the Savage Mine. He maintained his living quarters on the top two floors, with the lower floor devoted to the business of the company and serving as its assay office. Set into the hillside, the mansion has a fine Mansard roof ringed with a series of dormers and shows fine detailing on its street-level fence and on the ballustrade of the upstairs balcony. The current owners have proceeded room by room to restore the Victorian elegance of the Gold Rush era. All furnishings are in the Victorian style, including many of the original pieces that graced the superintendent's home, for example, the beds in the three guest rooms. The shared bathroom features the original copper bathtub and a functioning 1890 toilet. (The 1878 original is on display in the mansion as well.) The period carpeting and wall coverings carry through the Victorian theme. There are two parlors for use by the guests, some of whom frequently play the 1892 organ. Breakfast, served in the Victorian kitchen, is the only meal available at Savage Mansion. *Room Rates*: $40 for double rooms, including continental breakfast. *Pets*: Not permitted. *Driving Instructions*: Virginia City is reached by taking Route 17.

New Mexico

LIKE NEVADA, New Mexico bears evidence of human habitation that dates back more than 20,000 years. When white explorers came to the area they were greeted by the Pueblo Indians as well as Navaho, Apache, Ute, and Comanche tribesmen. The explorers came to New Mexico in the hopes of finding the treasure-laden Seven Cities of Cibola. Stories of the cities, never found, were perpetrated by the explorer Cabeza de Vaca, who had been shipwrecked near the Texas coast and had wandered across the southern territories, finally reaching the Pacific Coast. His stories led to dozens of exploratory parties including several to New Mexico. The first formal Spanish colony was settled in 1598 at Pueblo San Juan de los Caballeros. The governing offices were moved to Sante Fe in 1610, making that city the oldest seat of government in the country.

For the next eighty years there were periodic wars with the Pueblo Indians. The peace in 1692 was followed by a long period of uneventful Spanish rule. Mexico took control of New Mexico following Mexican independence in 1822. Mexican control ended in 1848, following the defeat of Mexico in the Mexican War. During the Civil War the region fell initially to the Confederacy but was quickly recaptured by the Union forces in 1862. Kit Carson and others led the effort to restrain the Navaho and Apache Indians, and peace was gradually established. New Mexico attained statehood in 1912.

Today, New Mexico, the Land of Enchantment, is the fifth largest state in the Union but has a population of only slightly more than one million. Tourism is a major source of revenue, and the state offers helpful travel information to those who write Tourist Division, Department of Development, 113 Washington Avenue, Santa Fe, NM 87503. The division may be reached toll-free at 800-545-9876.

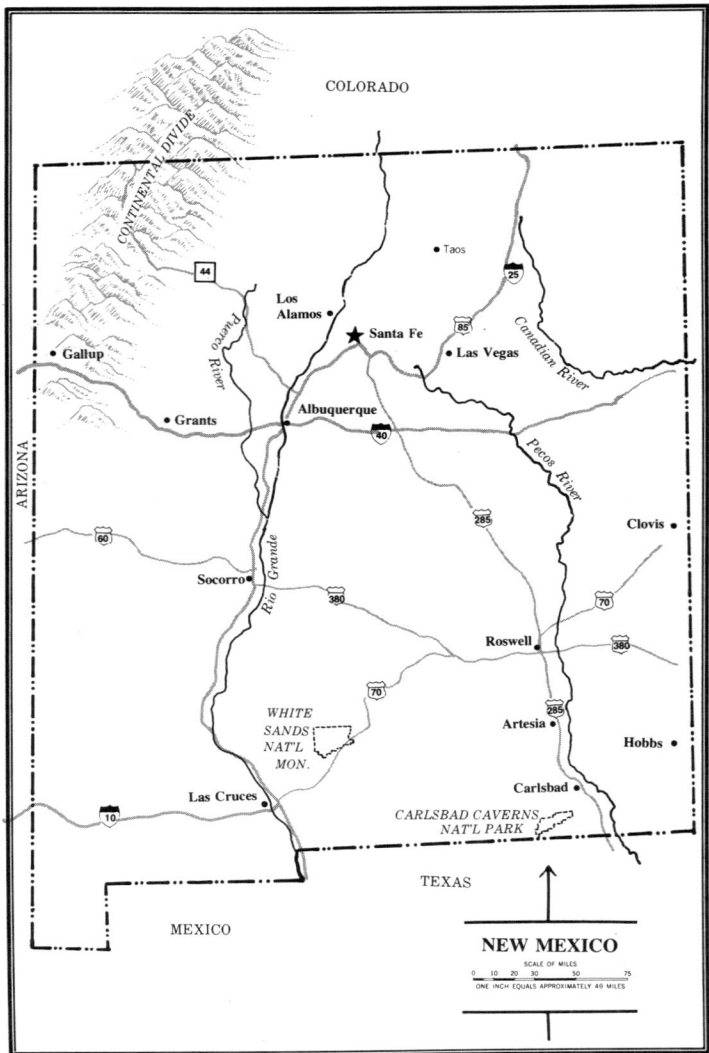

COLORADO

• Taos

Los Alamos •
★ Santa Fe
• Las Vegas

• Gallup

• Grants
Albuquerque

CONTINENTAL DIVIDE

Puerco River

Canadian River

Pecos River

Clovis •

Socorro •

Rio Grande

Roswell •

WHITE
SANDS
NAT'L
MON.

Artesia •

Hobbs •

Las Cruces •

Carlsbad •

CARLSBAD CAVERNS
NAT'L PARK

TEXAS

MEXICO

NEW MEXICO

SCALE OF MILES
0   10   20   30   50   75
ONE INCH EQUALS APPROXIMATELY 40 MILES

ARIZONA

Santa Fe, New Mexico

It sometimes comes as a shock to Easterners, but Santa Fe was already established as a seat of government ten years before the Pilgrims set foot on Plymouth Rock. On Santa Fe's historic plaza stands the *Palace of Governors*, the oldest public building in America. This historic plaza was once the site of one of Billy the Kid's brief episodes as a captive and housed a bull ring in the mid-nineteenth century. Today Pueblo Indians display their wares—pottery, jewelry, and homemade bread—daily. The Palace itself, built in 1610, was the seat of government for three hundred years. It is now a state museum.

Santa Fe has an abundance of beautiful churches from many periods. The *Mission of San Miguel* is an eighteenth-century church typical of New Mexico architecture. *St. Francis Cathedral*, of later construction, contains the oldest representation of the Madonna in this country. The *Loretto Chapel* contains an impressive circular staircase. Parts of the *Rosario Chapel* are believed to date to the late seventeenth century. One of the most important mission churches in the country is the late-eighteenth-century *Santuario de Guadalupe*, a repository for numerous examples of Spanish Colonial religious art and artifacts. Those interested in folk art should visit the *International Folk Art Museum* with its collection of art from fifty countries and the *Wheelright Museum*, which offers Indian-made articles. The *Old Cienega Village Museum* is a living museum depicting seventeenth- and eighteenth-century Spanish Colonial life on the grounds of the Rancho Las Golondrinas.

Many seasonal events are held in the Santa Fe area. Among the most important are the *Rodeo de Santa Fe*, which takes place over a four-day period in July. The *Santa Fe Fiesta* is a September festival of street dancing, balls, parades, historical pageants, religious ceremonies, and processions. The *Santa Fe Horse Show* is a three-day event held annually in August. Visits to the Indian pueblos in the area surrounding Santa Fe are a most important tourist attraction. The pueblos are the oldest cities in America. Be sure to ask permission to take pictures at all times, including during the very colorful ceremonial dancing. *The Santa Fe Opera Company* presents a summer season of opera under the stars featuring world-famous artists.

LA FONDA HOTEL

100 East San Francisco Street, Santa Fe, NM 87501. 505-982-5511. *Innkeeper*: Mrs. Dayle Pond. Open all year.

La Fonda is the Spanish term for "inn," and this one sits at the end of the Santa Fe Trail on a corner of the historic Plaza. There has been a *fonda* at this location since 1610, and the hotel has all the feel of an old adobe inn encrusted with the sands of time. In truth, the former adobe structure on this particular site died of old age in 1919. The current building, a 165-room hotel, was constructed in the soft-curved Spanish architectural style, with heavy timbers, dark woods, and tile floors. Its location at the end of the Santa Fe Trail and the rich history of the site combine to give a sense of the ages past in a setting that provides, as well, the comforts of a modern urban hotel. The list of guests who have stayed at the hotels located on this spot include General Grant, Rutherford B. Hayes, General Sherman, Billy the Kid, and an array of twentieth-century movie stars who have used the hotel as base while filming in the area.

This is not a small country inn, and guests can count on such city conveniences as air-conditioning, color television, and room telephones. Nevertheless, there is the ongoing effort here to provide an inn feeling through the Spanish room décor and little attentions to detail. At present the management of the hotel has installed traditional hand-carved and hand-painted Spanish furniture in about half the guest rooms. A series of fifth-floor suites has been recently redone with a fine selection of antiques that blend with the Spanish décor. All of the suites feature wood-burning fireplaces and balconies with views of the city and the mountains.

The main dining room, La Plazuela, is a glass-enclosed patio garden featuring Mexican food, prime ribs of beef, and other American specialties. Surrounding La Plazuela on the second-floor mezzanine are a variety of shops that supplement the many shops on the first floor. La Fonda is a city hotel, but it is somehow more innlike than most. *Room Rates*: Double rooms range from $31 to $48, depending on size and time of year. One-bedroom suites with fireplace and balcony are $75, and two-bedroom suites are $130. *Pets*: Permitted if small. *Driving Instructions*: Santa Fe is reached via I-25 from Albuquerque.

RANCHO ENCANTADO

Route 4, Tesuque, NM. Mailing address: Box 57-C, Sante Fe, NM 87501. 505-982-3537. *Innkeeper*: John T. Egan. Open from May 1 to October 31.

Rancho Encantado is a sprawling Southwestern ranch-inn. The main lodge and outlying buildings all appear to have been here since the first Conquistadores arrived. Not so: These low adobe and brick ranch-style houses were recently built, using the styles and materials traditional to the Southwest. The main lodge was built in the early 1920s, and the others quite a bit later. The energetic owner, Betty Egan, and her very talented family have completely transformed this formerly modest guest ranch into one of the finest resorts anywhere in the country.

The buildings stand against the backdrop of the Sangre de Cristo Mountains, and the 168-acre reach is encompassed almost entirely by the Santa Fe National Forest, rolling desert, and the Tesuque Indian Reservation. The views of the desert and distant hills are truly gorgeous. The big ranch lodge's five elegant guest rooms are up a natural tile-and-adobe staircase on the inn's top floor. The interiors of all the ranch's rooms and suites are quietly simple and elegant and look like old Western-movie sets, as well they should; much of the ranch has been used for just that purpose. The rooms have crisp white adobe walls, impressive wooden ceilings, open and high with massive exposed beams, and hand-made tiles everywhere. There are smooth, rounded adobe fireplaces and Franklin stoves in the guests' quarters. The furnishings are antiques from all over the world, blending with handsome Indian artifacts and woven rugs. The quarters range from intimate bedrooms to luxurious suites to complete housekeeping units. All the guest rooms have private baths.

The dining room and bar are on the ground floor of the main lodge. These rooms offer dining on several levels. As with all the rooms, handsome adobe walls, natural tiles, and wood-beamed high ceilings combine with the warm earth colors used throughout both in the Egans' choice of fabrics and leathers and in the many Indian weavings, artifacts, and rugs. The restaurant ranks as one of the finest in the West. It serves thick, juicy steaks and ribs, the traditional spicy foods of the Southwest and Mexico, and also Continental haute cuisine. Amazingly, the specialty at Rancho Encantado is fresh seafood; it is flown in from the coast every weekend, and there is a special seafood buffet on Friday nights to celebrate the flight.

The ranch maintains an excellent stable of horses and huge amounts of space in which to ride them. In addition to the horses, the resort ranch offers swimming, tennis, shuffleboard, and trap shooting. If you see people who look familiar, they probably are; this unique resort has been host to hundreds of world-famous personalities. Many come back to vacation at this beautiful spot where they slaved under hot lights and greasepaint as old Western heroes or villians. *Room Rates*: The rates were not available when this book went to press. *Driving Instructions*: Rancho Encantado is on Route 285, 8 miles north of downtown Santa Fe.

Taos Ski Valley (including Taos, New Mexico)

The valley is most famous as a ski resort. The *Taos Ski Valley* offers superb downhill and cross-country skiing in the high Sangre de Cristo Mountains 20 miles north of Taos. The ski area includes six chair lifts (some brand new—replacing the older lifts), two T-bars, and complete base facilities. The skiing is excellent from mid-November through mid-April. The *Taos Ski Valley Ski School* was founded by Bernard and Jean Mayer, two brothers who were members of the French Ski Team. At the end of May there is a week-long *Slalom Racing Camp* here. In summer there are tennis courts, horseback riding, and hiking available at the Hotel Edelweiss.

The *Carson National Forest*, with almost 1,500,000 acres of mountainous wilderness, offers unlimited hiking and backpacking opportunities, as well as fishing, Nordic skiing, and hunting. The mandatory wilderness permits are free and can be picked up at all

National Forest offices. The *Taos Ranger Station*'s phone numbers are 505-758-2911/2238. Here visitors can get permits, forest/wilderness trail maps (50¢), and backpacking and hiking information. Taos Ski Valley is host to students attending the *Taos School of Music*, and many student and faculty concerts are held in the summer months.

The town of Taos and the surrounding towns are renowned for their beauty. Artists and writers flock to the peaceful 7,000-foot-high town in the towering, rugged mountains. Just southeast of Taos Ski Valley is New Mexico's tallest peak, Wheeler (13,161 feet). The area is ringed by good, challenging ski areas. To the west of Taos, Route 64 crosses the deep, dark *Rio Grande Gorge* on a bridge 650 feet above the river. The river is wild and dangerous here. White water fans ride the rapids through the remote wilderness.

Taos itself is filled with historic sites and fine museums. The *Stables Gallery* features shows of famed Taos artists the year round. It is on North Pueblo Road. The first week in October the *Annual Taos Festival of the Arts* is held, featuring not only art work in various media but also dance, poetry readings, music, and drama.

Kit Carson's Home, Museum, and Memorial State Park are on Route 64 in town. Carson's grave is in the park, and the home and museum feature relics of the Spaniards and Indians and mementoes of the famous scout's life. It is open all year and charges a fee to adults.

Taos Pueblo is north of Taos. It is perhaps the most famous of all the remarkable Indian pueblos anywhere. The enormous structure is an architectural masterpiece of Indian workmanship. The Indians charge a small fee for cars and a larger fee for photos. This is truly a spectacular place and well worth the trip. At the end of September the tribe holds an *Annual San Geronimo Feast Day and Sundown Dance*. It features a trade fair, extraordinary ritual dances, foot races, and a pole climb.

HOTEL EDELWEISS

Box 83, Taos Ski Valley, NM 87571. 505-776-2301. *Innkeepers*: Bernard and Ilse Mayer. Open from June to September and December to April.

The Edelweiss is a Swiss chalet designed and built by Ilse Mayer and Bernard Mayer, a former member of a French Olympic ski team. The two bring a fine combination of French charm and European tradition to the hotel. The chalet is new, constructed in 1964 with a large addition in 1975. It has a warm and distinctive European flavor. The lodge is set in the heart of the town of Taos Ski Valley at the side of the beginners' slope. The big mountain slope rises up from the Edelweiss's door; it is possible to ski straight from the hotel to the nearby lifts.

The Edelweiss is actually two buildings, both built along traditional chalet lines, with big porches at ground level and small individual balconies at some of the upper-story windows. In summer months there are window boxes filled with bright flowers. Tall pines partially shade the two chalets and their porches. One building has a bright white stucco side with arch doorways set deep in the thick stone wall. The winter's wood supply is neatly stacked under the protective eaves of the steeply sloping roof. A zigzag post-and-rail fence borders the lodge, and the mountain seems to soar up from the yard. The other lodge is built of heavy logs above a white stucco base. The first two stories of the three-level hostelry have corner guest rooms with wraparound picture windows filling two whole walls of each room. The third-floor rooms open onto small balconies overlooking the slopes. The entrance to the chalet is another flower-bedecked porch (in summer) on which a guardian deer skull looks down from the crossbeam on the roof. Inside the buildings, the atmosphere is decidedly that of a European lodge with exposed ceiling beams; stuffed owls and hawks and elk and deer heads stare down from the lobby walls, and a roaring blaze can always be found in the large stone fireplace in the lounge. Comfortable couches and chairs abound. The inn's only television set (color) resides here in the guest's lounge. The big picture windows throughout the rooms offer views of the snow-covered slopes, skiers, and the big chair lifts in winter and the peaceful, grassy mountainside in summer. Hand-loomed wool rugs decorate the walls of the hallways.

The sixteen guest rooms are furnished with sturdy wooden furniture and comfortable beds. Each has a private bath. While the rooms are not actually bunk rooms, they come close; some have as many as five beds. Regular doubles and other combinations are available, though. The rooms with the big corner windows are magnificent.

The Edelweiss serves breakfasts in the dining room, where fresh flowers brighten the tables and the view from the wall of windows

is spectacular. The room, which doubles as the inn's greenhouse, is filled with all kinds of plants. The breakfasts are superb: Bernard is not only an expert skier but an enthusiastic chef. He personally cooks the elegant breakfasts of crepes with a variety of fillings and sauces. One day there will be banana blintzes, and the next, a wonderful French egg dish with fresh artichoke hearts, or whatever strikes Bernard's fancy. The other meals are served at the Hotel St. Bernard next door. This hotel, the only other in Taos Ski Valley, is run by Bernard's brother, Jean. The cooking at the St. Bernard is authentic French cuisine prepared by a French chef. The St. Bernard has a new rathskeller with entertainment and dancing every night. At the Edelweiss, which does not serve liquor, hot coffee and tea are always available and ice is provided. *Room Rates*: Winter rates from $20 per person for a four-bed room up to $30 per person for a double and $40 single, EP. Add $20 a day for all meals, if desired. There are many package rates, and some rooms have kitchens. Lift tickets and lessons are available. Summer room rates range from $20 single to $34 for a four-bed room. Three meals a day add $12 per person. Again, there are a variety of package plans. *Driving Instructions*: From Albuquerque take Routes 64 and 84N to Taos, about 150 miles. Taos Ski Valley is 20 miles north of Taos at the end of Route 150.

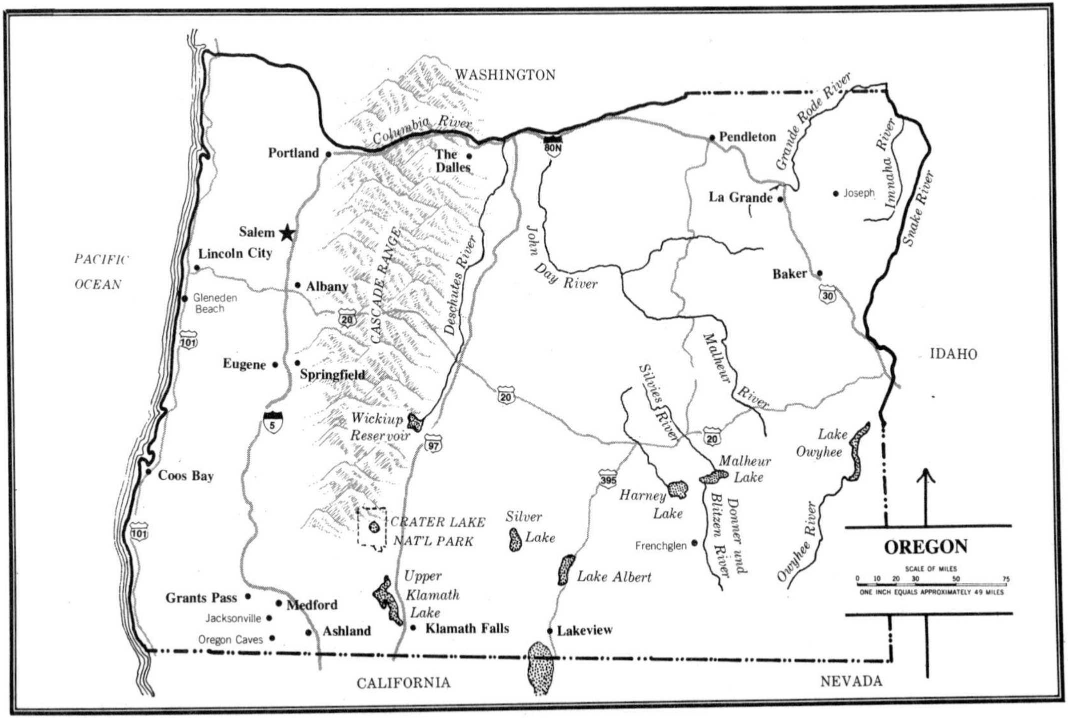
WASHINGTON
IDAHO
CALIFORNIA
NEVADA
PACIFIC
OCEAN
OREGON
SCALE OF MILES
0 10 20 30 50 75
ONE INCH EQUALS APPROXIMATELY 49 MILES
Columbia River
Grande Rode River
Imnaha River
Snake River
John Day River
Deschutes River
Malheur River
Silvies River
Donner und Blitzen River
Owyhee River
CASCADE RANGE
Portland
The Dalles
Pendleton
La Grande
Joseph
Baker
Salem
Lincoln City
Albany
Gleneden Beach
Eugene
Springfield
Wickiup Reservoir
Coos Bay
CRATER LAKE NAT'L PARK
Silver Lake
Harney Lake
Malheur Lake
Lake Owyhee
Frenchglen
Lake Albert
Upper Klamath Lake
Grants Pass
Medford
Jacksonville
Oregon Caves
Ashland
Klamath Falls
Lakeview
80N
30
20
101
5
97
395

Oregon

EARLY EXPLORATION OF the Oregon coastline was by Spanish explorers who had departed from Mexico en route to the Philippines in the sixteenth and seventeenth centuries. Sir Francis Drake ended his Pacific Coast exploration on the Oregon Coast, giving England some claim to the region. The first party to reach Oregon by land was the famous expedition led by Lewis and Clark. They reached the mouth of the Columbia River in 1805. In the first quarter of the nineteenth century, Russian settlers moved down the coast from Alaska, establishing settlements as far south as the Mendocino coast in California. These settlements threatened both the Spanish to the south and the English and American settlers. Treaties in the 1820s led to the eventual withdrawal of the Russians.

Oregon was a popular fur trading area, and the forested region attracted trappers and other settlers who traveled to Oregon via the Oregon Trail in the 1840s. Border disputes grew intense when Great Britain laid claim to much of Washington and Oregon based on claims established by the Hudson Bay Company, which was active there. These disputes led to James Polk's famous campaign slogan "Fifty-four Forty or Fight." The dispute was finally settled by compromise that established the forty-ninth parallel as the dividing point between English and American territories. Oregon was recognized as a territory in 1848, and statehood was granted in 1859. Statehood was followed by a series of wars between white settlers and several of the Northwestern Indian tribes.

Today, Oregon welcomes visitors to its "Alpine" slopes in the Cascade Mountains and the sand dunes of its coastline. It offers Shakespeare in the summer and warming mineral springs in the fall. For complete information on Oregon in all four seasons, write to the Oregon Department of Transportation, Travel Information, Salem, OR 97310.

Frenchglen, Oregon

Frenchglen is at the southern tip of the 180,000-acre *Malheur National Wildlife Refuge*, which stretches 40 miles northward along Route 205. The refuge, home for hundreds of species of birds, mammals, and other wildlife, is a major stop on the Pacific Flyway. To appreciate best the many natural wonders of the refuge, visitors should take the 42-mile self-guided auto tour of the Blitzen Valley, which runs the length of the refuge. Copies of the guide can be obtained at the refuge museum, about 30 miles north of the Frenchglen Hotel. The refuge is open daily all year. The *Harney County Fair and Rodeo* are held annually in early September at the fairgrounds in Burns, about 60 miles north of Frenchglen. About 17 miles east of Frenchglen is *Steens Mountain*, reached via unimproved secondary roads from the village. The mountain is a popular climbing spot with its summit at 9,670 feet, the highest in the region.

FRENCHGLEN HOTEL

Frenchglen, OR 97736. 503-493-2565. *Innkeeper*: Malena Konek. Open March 15 through December 15.

The Frenchglen Hotel is a tiny period piece that will appeal to those readers who appreciate old-fashioned accommodations in a restored turn-of-the-century hotel. The Frenchglen is owned by the Oregon State Parks System and operated under lease by Malena Konek. It is a homey place with a screened front veranda that is perfect for rocking on and chatting. The living room is equipped with an old upright piano with a guitar perched above it, ready for playing. There are books on the shelf for a late afternoon or evening read after a

day of hiking and exploring the nearby Malheur Wildlife Refuge. The guest rooms are small but comfortable, with new mattresses as the only concession to the decade. Each bed has a handmade quilt. The old practice of walking down the hall to the bathroom is in force for all eight guest rooms.

Dining here is similarly simple. The food is all home-cooked, and there is a single menu for the evening meal. All meals are typical country cooking served family style, usually accompanied by one of the several sourdough breads the hotel chef likes to make. The complete dinner was $6 in 1978 and the full breakfast was $3.25. *Room Rates* (1978): Rates are $16 to $19 per room. *Pets*: Not permitted. *Driving Instructions*: The inn is in Frenchglen, 60 miles south of Burns, Oregon, via Route 205.

Gleneden Beach, Oregon

Gleneden is a tiny community about 90 miles southwest of Portland on the Pacific Coast. Guests at the resort that follows will find life quite self-contained there and need not look to the surrounding villages for entertainment. However, one place to visit outside the resort is *Depoe Bay*, about 5 miles south of the resort, a picturesque harbor crammed with both commercial and private fishing vessels. Those who wish to may charter fishing boats to hunt the elusive Chinook salmon as well as cod, sea bass, and red snapper. The *Oregon State University Marine Center* at Newport offers displays and nature talks on the marine life of the Oregon coast. The coastline in the area is particularly scenic, and any number of shore drives may be undertaken from the town. There are several state parks within a short drive of Gleneden Beach.

SALISHAN LODGE

P.O. Box 118, Gleneden Beach, OR 97388. 503-764-2371. *Innkeeper*: Alex Murphy. Open all year.

Since Salishan opened in 1965, the resort complex has rapidly become one of the finest in the Northwest. The lodge comprises 150 guest rooms, several dining rooms, and other public areas, conference facilities, swimming pool, eighteen-hole golf course, three indoor tennis courts, and more than 3 miles of private beach. This bare-bones description makes it seem to be a place that greatly misses the mark of this book. Quite the contrary. Salishan is an exciting blend of contemporary architecture and the rugged beauty of the Oregon coastline. It is impossible, of course, to build a major resort in a remote and undeveloped area without disturbing the countryside at all. Here, however, the disturbance is minimized. This has been accomplished by spreading out the guest accommodations into relatively low-profile, two-story units and then, through careful use of landscaping, blending the man-made with the natural.

Guest rooms at Salishan are contemporary in design and filled with comforts that span the ages. Each room contains a fireplace, its own balcony, oversize beds, color television, individual temperature control, private bathroom, and covered parking at the door. The rooms blend wood and glass in a pleasing look with thin-slatted blinds, giving an Oriental feeling. It is in the use of wood that the lodge has excelled. Much of the warmth of the place is derived from the simple board-and-batten exterior that blends effortlessly with the use of wood on the interior. The fireplaces in the public areas are generally stone and in the guest rooms are brick.

The Salishan kitchen produces a selection of Continental and American food that has won plaudits from reviewers throughout the Northwest. Among its consistent awards are the Mobil Five Star rating and the listing in *Holiday Magazine* as one of the best in the country. The menu is pages long, with many standards of fine Continental-American cuisine present. The preparation of seafood and of some of the more unusual specialties is outstanding. From the list of appetizers one can pick salmon *mousse en gelée*, quenelles of sole in lobster sauce, or *koniginpastete* (a patty shell filled with sweetbreads, mushrooms, and veal in a cream sauce). From the twenty-eight entrées listed (plus specials of the day), a tiny sampling would include crabmeat "Pompadour" en casserole, fillet of sole Marguery, oven broiled chinook salmon, any of six steaks, rack of lamb, and more and more from lists that include numerous poultry, meat, and additional seafood dishes. The staff of resident chefs here will prepare many other dishes, including coulibiac of salmon, venison Baden-Baden, beef Wellington, and a cross-section of the finest of foods from virtually any ethnic and international cuisine, given forty-eight hours' advance notice.

Salishan is a complete resort that provides more than the ex-

pected golf, tennis, and swimming pools. The lodge has made a consistent effort to collect and display the works of Oregon artists in its public rooms and guest rooms. In addition, nature displays are found in cases mounted on the walls in the Sun Room Patio. These displays were prepared and supervised by the Oregon Museum of Science and Industry. The lodge is on more than 800 acres and has numerous walking trails that lead through the woods and down to the ocean front. Guests may walk, jog, or obtain special passes to drive to the parking area at the beach. *Room Rates*: Rates in 1978 were $38 to $59 without meals. *Driving Instructions*: The lodge is 6 miles south of Lincoln City on Route 101.

Jacksonville, Oregon

Jacksonville is an old mining town near the southern border of the state. It has survived relatively intact from its days as a prosperous gold town. The mid-1900s buildings stood untouched because of the town's isolation and its bypassing by the railroad in 1883. The *Jacksonville Museum*, open daily, houses local artifacts and the archives of the old Courthouse in town. The whole town is interesting. In addition to the many historic sites there are a great many antique and craft shops in and among the old Victorian buildings.

Just south of Jacksonville is the open air *Peter Britt Music Festival*, held for two weeks in mid-August annually. The festival features outdoor concerts, chamber music, recitals, chorale music, and youth and band concerts held in the huge new open pavilion in the Peter Britt Gardens. For information write Box 669, Jacksonville, OR 97530 or phone after August 1, 503-899-1821. Swimming and fishing are offered on the nearby *Applegate River*. North of Jacksonville on Route 238 is the *Rogue River*, creator of this magnificent Rogue Valley. The *Valley of the Rogue State Park* is off I-5 to the north. The rugged river offers excellent fishing for steelhead and trout. It is one of the most popular rivers in the West and even has special Rogue River boats designed for use on it. Rafting trips are available in the towns nearby. To the southwest on Route 43 is *Oregon Caves National Monument*, discovered in 1874, with underground formations of memorable beauty. The surrounding area is lovely also, with towering trees clinging to high, rugged mountainsides. Hiking is excellent throughout this corner of Oregon.

Ashland, south of Medford, is host to the *Oregon Shakespearean Festival* with its two seasons (February through April, weekends only in April and May; and the Shakespeare Summer, June through September). The festival has three theaters and ten productions. A great variety of plays are performed here each season in addition to Shakespearean productions. Special barbecues and traditional feasts are held throughout the season. Call 503-482-2111 or ticket offices throughout California, Washington, and Oregon.

JACKSONVILLE INN

175 East California Street, Jacksonville, OR. Mailing address: P.O. Box 359, Jacksonville, OR 97530. 503-899-1900. *Innkeeper*: Jerry Evans. Open all year.

Jacksonville is Oregon's first Gold Rush town. Much of the town's classic mid-nineteenth-century architecture survived unscathed by modernization because of its isolation. The town is now on the National Registry of Historic Districts. One of the first permanent brick buildings (1863) in the boom town was the Jacksonville Hotel, constructed of local bricks and hand-hewn sandstone from the local quarries and the old Jacksonville brick kiln. The sturdy two-story hotel was owned by two enterprising merchants named Ryan and Morgan, who sold just about everything a miner or his lady could possibly want, from medicines and clothing to hardware and groceries. The building has taken many shapes and forms since then; for a while it was a bank, then a hardware store, and finally the present hotel and restaurant. The hotel had several wooden stories for a few years, but they are long gone.

The walls of the dining room are exposed sandstone, and the mortar still has flecks of gold glinting in it. This room has been totally redone, and it is attractive though not a replica of the original. The innkeeper used beautiful worn panels of wood rescued from an early hotel being demolished. The heavy timbers came from a turn-of-the-century sawmill. Dinners are served by candlelight in the stone-and-brick-walled room warmed by a crackling fire in the old timber-mantled brick fireplace. The menu features Continental cuisine. In season the chef offers fresh salmon and razor clams pan-fried in butter. The specialties of the house are veal dishes from old family recipes of the chef's and prime ribs au jus. All meals are either à la carte—with salad, rice or baked potato, and fresh vegetables—or complete dinners with marinated beans and relishes, an appetizing wine, hot fresh breads, a pasta course, vegetables, dessert, and coffee. There is an extensive wine list to complement the meal. The hotel serves only dinners, but several restaurants within walking distance serve good breakfasts and lunches. A lounge is adjacent to the restaurant with a bar and live folk music on Friday and Saturday evenings.

The hotel's eight guest rooms can be reached via a partially covered rough-hewn staircase lighted by old lanterns and constructed out of whipsawed lumber from a 1905 structure. The air-conditioned

rooms have private baths and are decorated with fine old local antiques re-creating the colorful atmosphere of the old West. The furnishings come from that elegant era of the Gold Rush. There are heavy oak bedsteads, antique brass beds, and period dressers and rockers, surrounded by old brick walls. *Room Rates*: Singles are $18 (EP); doubles are $23; and one extra-large room with two double beds is $25 for two. Additional guests are $2 each. *Driving Instructions*: From Medford, about 30 miles north of the California border on I-5, take Route 238 west 5 miles to Jacksonville.

Joseph, Oregon

Joseph is in the northeast corner of Oregon on the north shore of beautiful Wallows Lake. This area is considered the gateway to the "Northwest's Switzerland." The Wallowa Mountains rise majestically behind the lake and town. The mountains were once the hunting grounds of the Nez Percé Indians under the powerful rule of Chief Joseph. The Wallowa River valley was the Indians' homeland, and they were the last of the tribes defeated by the army, but not before a brave and mighty struggle that covered thousands of miles. The chief is buried at the north side of the lake. *Chief Joseph Days Rodeo* is held the last weekend in July in Joseph. South of the lake is the *Mount Howard Gondola Lift*, the steepest and longest four-passenger gondola in the United States. The ride carries passengers from the lake to the summit of the 8,200-foot Mount Howard, at a vertical rise of 690 feet a minute. From the summit visitors have spectacular views of the Wallowa Valley, the incredible Eagle Cap wilderness of the Wallowa Mountains and the rugged canyons of the Imnaha and Snake rivers. The deer are quite tame here, and elk and bear are often seen from the summit. The meadows are covered with wildflowers.

The *Eagle Cap Area* is one of the most remote wildernesses in the Northwest. The area encompasses more than 200,000 acres of towering 8,000- and 10,000-foot mountains and many untouched alpine lakes of unsurpassed beauty. In Joseph the Eagle Cap Station will provide visitors with information on the many types of wilderness tours and facilities available. There are guided tours by horseback or on foot, and the trails are well marked for independent travel. From

Wallowa Lake Lodge there are one-day trips overland on Forest Service roads to Hell's Canyon. From *Hat Point Lookout* on the canyon's rim, one looks down on a gorge whose depth exceeds that of the Grand Canyon by 2,000 feet. The town of Joseph has many of the more prosaic recreational activities, such as golf (miniature and regulation), roller skating, and go-carts riding.

WALLOWA LAKE LODGE

Box I, Joseph, OR 97846. 503-432-4082 or 432-2484. *Innkeepers*: The Wiggins family. Open June 15 to September 15; cabins available May 1 to September 30.

Wallowa Lake Lodge is an old rustic hotel on the south shore of beautiful Wallowa Lake, within view of some of this country's highest, most rugged mountains. The hotel is nestled among towering pines and shady lawns between the crystal clear lake and the snow-capped mountains.

Below the main lodge are several log cabins with fireplaces and housekeeping facilities. The lodge is a large, dark brown wooden structure with an enormous fieldstone chimney on one side. The chimney connects with an imposing stone fireplace in the spacious lounge inside. The lounge has comfortable old furniture and plenty of table games and amusements for rainy days and evenings. The hotel is, Mrs. Wiggins says, a "real antique." This feeling comes from its untouched quality: It has no restored rooms, refinished heirloom furniture, or color-coordinated décor, just a comfortable country hotel with its 1920s furnishings and accompanying atmosphere. The twenty-one guest rooms on the second and third floors are much the same as when the lodge was built. Each pair of rooms has an adjoining bathroom with either a shower or tub. Many of the rooms themselves contain washbasins.

The lodge's dining room is open to guests and the public for breakfasts and dinners. The hearty meals are designed to assuage the biggest of fresh mountain air appetites. The menu features plenty of traditional American fare. The kitchen will make up box lunches if requests are made at breakfast time. Drinks are served in the dining room and downstairs in the Nez Percé Cocktail Lounge.

The lodge offers complete lakeside facilities, including a launching area and rentals of boats, motors, canoes, and water bikes. The Wallowa Lake State Park adjoins the lodge, and the two combine to provide a wide assortment of recreational activities. The lake provides swimming, boating, and fishing, while the park has excellent marked hiking trails, playground areas, and camping facilities. There are nature talks and guided tours of the area. Horseback riding is available in Joseph with full pack trips of three hours or longer into the Alpine lake regions. This is an area of breathtaking scenery, and the Wallowa Lake Lodge is a great place to make home base for a stay. *Room Rates*: The rates were unavailable for 1979 but are approximately in the range of $14 single to $30 for a suite in the lodge itself, EP, and the cabins are in the same range. *Pets*: Not permitted. *Driving Instructions*: From Pendleton, almost 130 miles west of Joseph, take Route 80N east to La Grande and then Route 82 to Joseph, the lodge is 6 miles south of town. From Idaho (Boise) take Route 80N west to La Grande and Route 82 to Joseph and then 6 miles south along the lake. There is a private plane landing strip in Joseph and another 12 miles away in Enterprise.

Mount Hood (including Government Camp, Oregon)

Mount Hood dominates the sky here. The 11,235-foot mountain was once an active volcano, and a climb to its summit will reveal a still-smoking crater. The mountain is Oregon's highest and provides year-round skiing and hiking. There are several ski areas operating on the mountain. Timberline Lodge, described below, has complete base facilities, and snow cats carry skiers and sightseers almost to the summit. *Government Camp Ski Area* is another popular area serving the mountain. Both facilities share the 8-mile ski run, the country's longest. Cross-country skiing is available at most ski areas. Timberline holds ski races throughout the year.

To the north of Government Camp along Route I-80N is *Multnomah Falls*, the highest of the many cascades along the Columbia Gorge. The falls drop an awesome 620 feet. The upper scenic route parallels the river-level I-80N on the Columbia River Gorge. There are many breathtaking waterfalls, and eleven are major falls of incredible height. At the Bonneville Dam, 39 miles east of Portland, are the fish ladders built for the runs of salmon, steelhead, and other spawning migratory fish.

TIMBERLINE LODGE

Government Camp, OR 97028. 503-272-3311. *Innkeeper*: Richard
L. Kohnstamm. Open all year.

Timberline Lodge is the pride of Oregon. This old giant was one of
Franklin D. Roosevelt's WPA Projects in the midst of the Depression; the President himself dedicated the building in 1937. The lodge
is a work of art; its mammoth structure with the 100-foot-high, 400-
ton chimney stands as a proud testament to the Oregon men and
women who built and furnished it. The chimney and massive fireplaces were fashioned out of volcanic rocks from the still-smoking
Mount Hood. The lodge was constructed by hundreds of Oregonians
who were taught stonemasonry, blacksmithing, carving, and building
by local artisans and imported Old World craftsmen.

Throughout the lodge are fine works of art in a variety of media,
all hand-crafted by local people from materials of the region. The
heavy hardwood chairs and tables were hand-hewn and held together
with iron straps and rugged rawhide seating. Telephone poles were
sawed off and beautifully carved as newel posts on the enormous
stairways and as posts on the balustrades of the many balconies both
inside and out. The lodge maintains several themes in its varied
décor. There are signs, carvings, paintings, weavings, metalwork,
and stained glass depicting pioneers, Indians, and the wildlife of
Oregon. The newel posts were intricately carved in the shapes of
animals and birds of the area. There are also paintings of the flora
and fauna and weavings representing the Indians. The Blue Ox Bar

on the lower level is decorated with stained-glass murals portraying Paul Bunyan and his ox, Babe.

The fifty-three guest rooms are on several floors in the spreading wings of the lodge off the main section. The furnishings and décor have an unusual handsome strength and beauty where the simplicity of the 1930s designs and the colorful hand-hooked rugs and appliqué bedspreads and drapes blend with the soft warmth of the blond woods. Richard Kohnstamm, the innkeeper for more than two decades here, has, with many Oregon residents, organized "Friends of the Timberline." These "Friends" repair and replace the worn furnishings with perfect reproductions true to the original work in order to preserve the craftsmanship of the men and women who devoted so much to the lodge's beginnings. The rooms are lighted by the hand-wrought chandeliers and bedside lamps. Four of the large rooms have fireplaces. Each has its own private bath. The guest rooms offer lodgers some of the most breathtaking views to be found anywhere. Some look out on the slopes of the towering Mount Hood; others overlook the valley below.

The lodge maintains a skiers' restaurant on the lower level as well as the Blue Ox Bar. On the third-floor balcony overlooking the tremendous second-floor lobby is the Ram's Head Bar, opening out to balconies over the valley below. On the second floor is the Cascadian Dining Room, heated by several of the inn's gigantic fireplaces. The menu here, with meals served all day, features hearty traditional American fare, the specialty being fresh salmon.

The Timberline Lodge, as the name implies, sits at the timberline (6,000 feet above sea level) on the slope of Oregon's highest mountain, Mount Hood. The four-story lodge blends beautifully with the mountain above, and it overlooks the majestic valley to distant Mount Jefferson beyond. The mountain provides year-round skiing; hundreds of thousands of skiers have passed through the ski lodge in Timberline's lower level, warmed by a crackling fire in the huge bottom-floor hearth of the towering stone chimney. In addition to the excellent, modern ski facilities here there are ski shops, gift shops, saunas, and a heated outdoor pool. Timberline Lodge is a place that everyone should see at least once in a lifetime. *Room Rates*: Rates range from $31 to $60 for a double, lower for singles, E.P. *Pets*: not permitted. *Driving Instructions*: From Portland take I-80N east for a short way, watching for signs to Route 26 at Wood Village. Stay on

Route 26 going east to Government Camp. There will be well-marked signs to the lodge. It is 60 miles from Portland.

Oregon Caves, Oregon

The *Oregon Caves National Monument* is located at 4,000 feet in the rugged, timber-covered Siskiyou Mountains. The 480-acre national monument features a vast water-formed cavern deep inside a mountain of marble. The caves are beautiful, and guided tours for small groups of people are available all year long. Fees are $2.50 for adults and $1.75 and $1.25 for children over six (those under six years are not allowed in the cave). Babysitting is provided at $1.25 per child.

On Labor Day weekends, the town has a *Logger's Jubilee Celebration* sponsored by the Lion's Club. At the *Siskiyou Smoke Jumper's Base*, 2 miles south of Cave Junction on the Redwood Highway, visitors can watch the firefighters' training sessions. *Bolan Lake and the Siskiyou National Forest Campgrounds* are southeast of Cave Junction and offer hiking and fishing as well as camping. *Kerby* is the next town north of Cave Junction on Route 199. It has a *Pioneer Museum* and a *"ghost town."* Route 199 goes along the Smith's River as it winds through the famed redwood giants to the sea near Crescent City, California. The Route, known as the *Redwood Highway*, runs 75 miles from Cave Junction to the sea.

OREGON CAVES CHATEAU

Oregon Caves, OR. Mailing address: P.O. Box 151, Grants Pass, OR 97526. 503-476-2534. *Innkeeper*: Charles Quigley. Open June 15 through September 8.

Oregon Caves National Monument and the Chateau are in the heart of the Siskiyou Mountains in the southwestern corner of the state at an altitude of 4,000 feet. In 1874, hunter Elijah Davidson followed his dog Bruno into the mouth of a moss-covered cave hot on the trail of a bear. Thus were the beautiful "Marble Halls of Oregon" discovered. Explorers came and went, but it wasn't until 1909 that President William Howard Taft proclaimed a tract of 480 acres the Oregon Caves National Monument. There is really only one cave. The area in and around it is of great natural beauty and has attracted millions of tourists over the years. In 1934, the Oregon Chateau, a rustic lodge, was built to accommodate some of the visitors. Situated on a mountain wall, it rises six majestic stories from the canyon floor. The rough natural-wood lodge blends beautifully with the towering pines, the steep mountainside, and the moss-covered marble cliffs.

Visitors enter the Chateau on the fourth floor, where the big doorway opens onto the steep mountain roadway. The fourth floor has a narrow little exterior walkway alongside of the building. Inside the huge wood-paneled lobby is an enormous double fireplace of rough cut marble blocks hewn from the mountain. The large picture windows look out into the treetops and down to the canyon below. The waterfall can be seen from here, the sound of its rushing waters joining that of the wind in the trees to fill the rooms with the soothing voice of wilderness nature. The public rooms throughout the Chateau are constructed of exposed hand-hewn pine beams of incredible thicknesses, supported by mammoth tree trucks, their sides smoothed by time and the touch of many hands. Much of the original 1930s furniture has been replaced, but the old handcrafted hanging chandeliers and some of the hand-made iron-strap furniture remains. The inn has been updated with new plumbing and wall-to-wall carpeting, but the rustic European atmosphere is still here. Most of the rooms have breathtaking views of the forest wilderness—the trees, canyon, and waterfalls. Each of the forty guest rooms has a private bath.

On the third-floor landing, overlooking the dining room, guests hear the "musical falls," the mountain stream as it comes over the falls and flows on through the dining room itself and on out to the sea 75 miles away. The dining room, divided by the stream, serves three meals a day in this rustic sunny picture-windowed room with its views of more gorgeous scenery. All the meals are reasonably priced.

The Oregon Chateau also has a nearby cottage in the same style as the big inn. *Room Rates*: The rates are approximately $12 to $15 for a single and $15 to $20 for a double (EP). Family units are slightly higher. *Pets*: Not permitted. *Driving Instructions*: Take Route 199 50 miles down from Grants Pass to Cave Junction, then turn east on Route 46 and go 20 miles to the national monument. From Crescent City on the California coast take Route 199 north 26 miles to get to Cave Junction.

Utah

THE FIRST SETTLERS of Utah were, of course, native American Indians, primarily pueblo- and cliff-dwellers. In more recent years, much of the area was occupied by the Navaho tribe, as well as the smaller Paiute, Ute, and Shoshone tribes. The first known exploration of the region was by two Spanish monks in 1776. Fifty years passed before the trapper Jim Bridger set foot on the shores of Great Salt Lake. Development of the region was accomplished by Mormons seeking religious freedom under the leadership of Brigham Young. Young and his followers arrived at Great Salt Lake in 1847. The ensuing years saw a series of wars between the settling Mormons and the tribes native to the region, who resented being displaced by the newcomers. A war of particular ferocity was waged by Chief Black Hawk of the Ute tribe, lasting from 1865 to 1867.

Originally part of the Mexican claim of vast holdings in the West, the territory that included Utah was ceded to the United States after the Mexican War ended in 1848. Statehood was proposed several times in the years following the Mexican treaty, but in each case a distaste in Congress for the polygamy practiced by the Mormons prevented the granting of requests for statehood. In the meantime, the Golden Spike had been driven at Promontory, Utah, linking the East and West coasts with a unified railway system. Railway development began in earnest soon thereafter in Utah, and the pleas for statehood continued. Finally, in 1890 the Mormon church passed a law prohibiting polygamy (already a federal offense since 1862), and this led to the admission of Utah as a state five years later.

Tourists planning to visit Utah should ask the state for useful travel information prior to leaving. Write the Utah Travel Council, Council Hall, Capital Hill, Salt Lake City, UT 84114, or call 801-533-5681.

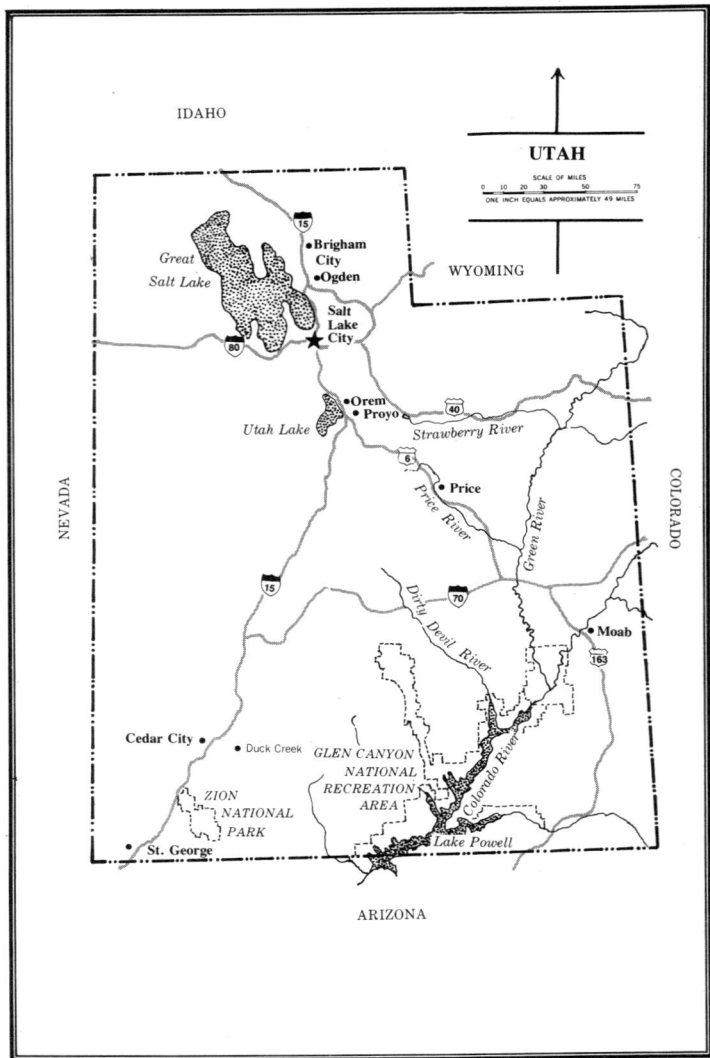

IDAHO

UTAH

SCALE OF MILES
0   10   20   30   50   75
ONE INCH EQUALS APPROXIMATELY 49 MILES

WYOMING

Great
Salt Lake

●Brigham
City
●Ogden

★Salt
Lake
City

●Orem
Provo●

Utah Lake

Strawberry River

●Price

Price River

Green River

Dirty Devil River

●Moab

Cedar City ●

● Duck Creek

GLEN CANYON
NATIONAL
RECREATION
AREA

Colorado River

ZION
NATIONAL
PARK

●St. George

Lake Powell

NEVADA

COLORADO

ARIZONA

Duck Creek, Utah

Duck Creek is an area—not really a community—about 30 miles east of Cedar City in the heart of the Dixie National Forest. It is a comfortable drive away from *Bryce National Park* (50 miles), *Zion National Park* (50 miles), and *Cedar Breaks National Monument* (15 miles). The area, like most of Utah, is a bonanza for photographers, hikers, artists, and fishermen. There is good local fishing for several kinds of trout at Navajo Lake and Duck Pond as well as stream fishing in Mammoth Creek, Asay Creek, and Sevier River. Mineral hunting is popular, with geodes and petrified wood among the prized local finds. In the winter, the national forest permits cross-country skiing and snowmobiling over a variety of trails and across a wide range of terrains from the mountains to the plateau meadows. The *Utah Shakespearean Festival* at Southern Utah State College in Cedar City is held annually during July and August.

MEADEAU VIEW LODGE

Utah Highway 14 at Meadeau View Movie Ranch, Duck Creek, UT. Mailing Address: P.O. Box 356, Cedar City, UT 84720. 801-648-2495. *Innkeepers:* Harry and Gaby Moyer. Open all year.

Meadeau View is a small (six guest rooms and three suites) lodge constructed in 1964. A peeled-log exterior combines with low, wood-shingled roofs to blend harmoniously into the seemingly unending wilderness surrounding the lodge. Meadeau View is in a handsome setting 8,400 feet above sea level among aspens, pines, and wildflowers. The interior carries out the warm wood tones with an abundance of pine paneling and recently installed carpeting in all rooms. The regular guest rooms are on the lower level of the two-story lodge building, and the suites are above. Regular rooms feature various combinations of queen, double, and twin beds. Some have French doors. The suites upstairs are large, with dormer windows that overlook the surrounding meadow. Each has a queen-size bed, pull-down divan, and complete modern bathroom. The lodge lobby has a geode-faced circular fireplace with swivel chairs around it for lounging.

The lodge is in the midst of the Dixie National Forest, and it is for enjoyment of this scenic area that most guests come. Meals in the lodge are simple, family-style affairs featuring homemade breads and rolls and an entrée of the day such as filet mignon, chicken in wine sauce, or homemade noodles with spaghetti sauce. *Room Rates:* Double rooms are $22 to $26 per day. Singles are less, and extra people are $4 per day. No charge for children under five years of age. *Pets:* Only small, house-trained pets that remain the guests' full responsibility are considered for acceptance. *Driving Instructions:* The lodge is 30 miles east of Cedar City on Route 14. It is 11 miles west of the intersection of Routes 14 and 89.

Monument Valley, Utah

Monument Valley, bestriding the Utah-Arizona border, is a region bedecked with spires, cave ruins, natural rock archways, buttes, mesas, and ancient cliff dwellings. It is in the northern portion of a vast Navaho reservation. Tours are conducted daily through the area under the leadership of bilingual Navaho drivers, who transport visitors to the sights of the region in air-conditioned four-wheel-drive vehicles. The *Valley Tour* leaves from Monument Pass and travels among the buttes to stops at Indian camps and the ruins of the ancient valley peoples. The *Mystery Valley Tour* passes by sand-softened archways, caves, and hidden canyons. The tour includes stops at two ancient dwellings, Babt House and Honeymoon House. The *Hoskinnini Mesa Tour* offers views of the buttes and mesas of the surrounding valley from a remote and picturesque mesa. Some of the tour passes through Indian camps, cornfields, and flocks of sheep and goats. Cliff dwellings are visited, and the fossil prints of prehistoric animals may be seen.

Visitors to the land of the Navaho frequently wish to purchase some of the Indians' beautiful jewelry. This can be risky for the unwary tourist. It is always best to limit shopping to places with established reputations as dealers. One such place is the *Navaho Arts and Crafts Guild* in Monument Valley. Information on touring and shopping in Monument Valley is available at and arranged through Goulding's Trading Post described below.

GOULDING'S TRADING POST AND LODGE

Box 1, Monument Valley, UT 84536. 801-727-3231. *Innkeeper:* John R. Burden. Open March 15 to November 1.

Within the Navaho's Tribal Park in Monument Valley is the Goulding's Trading Post and Lodge. The buildings and lodges of earth colors and clays are nearly invisible from even a short distance; save for the glint of windows reflecting the sky. The trading post and lodge sprawl across a sandstone bench on the side of a mesa overlooking Monument Valley. Behind the lodge rises the 1,000-foot sheer wall of one of the monuments. The motel-like lodge has nineteen units, each bright and cheerful but very simply funished; however, even the plushest, most elegant of rooms would pale beside the magnificence of the valley spread before it. Visible from every window are scenes of enchantment. The rooms here are all air-conditioned and heated. Each has two double beds and private bath. The first of the rooms were built to house the crews and performers of the booming movie business in the valley. The location is a favorite among producers of Western films and commercials. The first movie made here was John Ford's *Stagecoach* (1939).

Today Goulding's maintains the guest rooms, a trading post, and several stores for their nearby KOA Campground. All meals at the Lodge are served ranch style in the informal dining room. All the meals feature hearty Southwestern fare and are reasonably priced. Breakfasts and lunches are about $3.75, and complete dinners cost a mere $6.95. No liquor is sold here, because federal law prohibits the sale of alcoholic beverages on the reservation. The lodge will provide setups and ice for guests who bring their own liquor. All meals are available to the public with advance reservations.

The Trading Post was opened by the Gouldings in 1923 for trade with the Navaho on their reservation. It is still very much in operation today. It sells a wide variety of authentic Indian jewelry, baskets, rugs, and other Indian crafts. Mr. and Mrs. Goulding have generously donated the lodge, trading post, and 640 acres of land in Monument Valley to Knox College in Galesburg, Illinois. The profits from the operation go toward scholarships for Navaho students attending Knox. In addition, the college, through the Gouldings, has given the Seventh-Day Adventist Church a 99-year lease to run a hospital for the Navaho here. *Room Rates:* Rooms range from $23 for a single to $31 for four people. *Driving Instructions:* The lodge is on the border of Utah and Arizona off Route 163. It is on a small, marked road to the west, 22 miles north of Kayenta, Arizona, and 22 miles south of Mexican Hat, Utah. There is a landing strip for small planes here (UNICOM 122 8, Monument Valley).

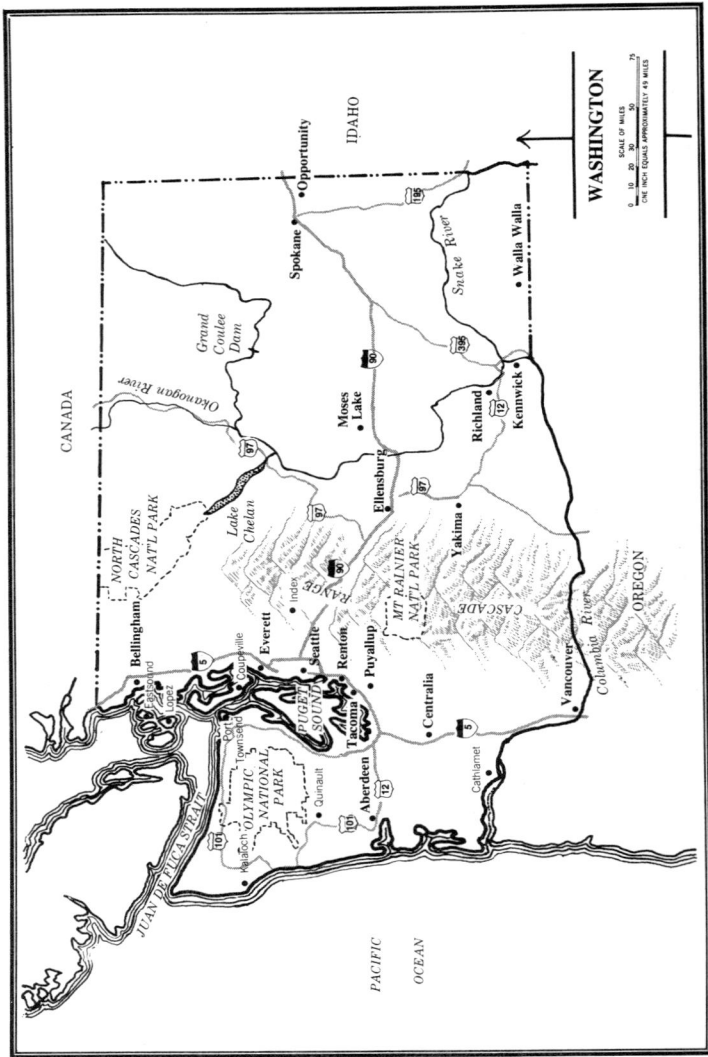

WASHINGTON

SCALE OF MILES
0 10 20 30   50   75
ONE INCH EQUALS APPROXIMATELY 49 MILES

CANADA

IDAHO

OREGON

PACIFIC OCEAN

JUAN DE FUCA STRAIT

PUGET SOUND

NORTH CASCADES NAT'L PARK

OLYMPIC NATIONAL PARK

MT RAINIER NAT'L PARK

CASCADE RANGE

Okanogan River

Snake River

Columbia River

Grand Coulee Dam

Lake Chelan

Opportunity
Spokane
Walla Walla
Moses Lake
Kennewick
Richland
Ellensburg
Yakima
Bellingham
Everett
Seattle
Renton
Puyallup
Tacoma
Centralia
Vancouver
Aberdeen
Cathlamet
Coupeville
Port Townsend
Quinault
Index

Lopez
San Juan

5
90
97
12
395
195
101

Washington

ALTHOUGH THERE WAS SOME early exploration of the Washington region by both Spanish and English explorers early in the eighteenth century, the first extensive recorded exploration of the coast was by Captain George Vancouver from 1792 to 1794. He explored Puget Sound (named for one of his chief officers) in detail during this period. This exploration led to an early English claim, reinforced by the domination of the area by English fur traders, especially those from the Hudson Bay Company, which had set up a protected trading post at Fort Vancouver on the Columbia River. As United States settlers established their settlements in Washington, there was mounting tension over the U.S.-Canadian border. This led to the famous "Fifty-four Forty or Fight" slogan of James Polk. Ultimately the dispute was settled by the treaties that established the forty-ninth parallel as the border. In 1853 Millard Filmore established the Washington Territory with its capital at Olympia. Statehood (as the forty-second state) followed in 1889. Irrigation in the years that followed opened much of the formerly unusable land in the eastern half of the state to agriculture. The state today is a major producer of apples and has a large lumber and paper industry.

Travelers to Washington should write for travel information to the Department of Commerce and Economic Development, Travel Development Division, General Administration Building, Olympia, WA 98504, or call 206-753-5000.

Cathlamet, Washington

Cathlamet is in Wahkiakum County at the southern edge of the State of Washington on the Columbia River, which forms the border with Oregon. The town is about 75 miles northwest of Portland. Cathlamet has a population of about 650 and is the site of the *County Museum* and the *Annual Logging Show* held in mid-July. This show attracts woodsmen from all over the Northeast to compete in high-climbing, log-bucking, and axe-throwing contests. Neighboring Skamokawa is the site of a most unusual *Round Barn*, the *Columbian White-tailed Deer Refuge*, and *Redmen Hall*. And the *Wahkiakum County Fair* held annually for more than seventy years. There is an annual *free* salmon barbecue at the fair every August. Route 4 runs along the Columbia River and offers motorists a gentle and scenic introduction to southern Washington.

CATHLAMET HOTEL

67-69 Main Street, Cathlamet, WA 98612. 206-795-8751 and 206-795-3997. *Innkeepers:* Pierre and Claire Pype. Open all year; restaurant open Wednesday through Sunday only.

When Pierre Pype first saw the old Cathlamet Hotel in 1974, it had slipped into disrepair from its handsome origins. A lifelong lover of old buildings, he determined almost immediately to save the basically sound building. He fetched his wife and ten children from their suburban Chicago home and set about the monumental task of renovating and restoring the hotel. The guiding rule has been to re-create the feeling of 1927, the year the hotel was built, and to retain as many of the original furnishings and fixtures as possible.

The hotel required complete repainting and wallpapering, but the original goal to keep the flavor of the period was admirably met. To the original lighting and furniture that remained, the new innkeeper added an extensive collection of antiques that include period upholstered lounge furniture and a set of white wicker installed in the upstairs lobby, which has a large stained-glass window. Decorative touches are pleasant and often amusing: A fireman's hat adorns the men's bathroom, and a pair of high button shoes graces the ladies' room. The overall effect here lies somewhere between a country home and a small hotel. The thirteen guest rooms largely adhere to the 1920s fashion of having connecting or hall bathrooms, although one has its own private bath.

The Pypes purchased a connecting 1890s Victorian home and redecorated it to make the cheery and very popular Pierre's Restaurant. Henri De Jonghe was a great uncle of Pype's, and the dish he created, Shrimp De Jonghe, is as much of a hit at this gourmet restaurant as it was at the De Jonghe Hotel in Chicago in the 1890s. Other specialties of the house include locally caught salmon, a variety of Washington seafood, pan-fried oysters, chicken Cordon Bleu, and filet Wellington. The food is often the attraction that brings visitors to Cathalmet, and the hotel turns out to be a pleasant bonus. In addition to dinner, the hotel/restaurant serves a large continental breakfast daily and a brunch on Sundays. *Room Rates:* Singles are $10 to $13 and doubles are $15 to $17, including continental breakfast served in the guest rooms. *Driving Instructions:* Take the Longview Kelso exit from I-5, Ocean Beach Highway , Route 4, west 25 miles to Cathlamet Junction, Route 409, and go left approximately four blocks to the hotel.

Coupeville, Washington

Coupeville is one of several small villages on Whidbey Island, a 50-mile-long island that lies in Puget Sound separating the state of Washington from Vancouver Island, Canada. Because the island was under seige by local Indians in its early period of settlement in the 1850s, a series of blockhouses were built. Some survive today, as do a number of restored buildings in the village dating from the 1870s. The village is listed as a Preserved Historic Town by the State of Washington. The island may be reached at its southern end by car ferry from Mukilteo on the mainland or by road (Route 20) from its northern end near Anacortes. Parts of the early fortifications remain today at *Fort Casey State Park*, 3 miles south of the village.

THE CAPTAIN WHIDBEY

2072 West Whidbey Island Inn Road, Coupeville, WA. Mailing address: Route 1, Box 32, Coupeville, WA 98329. 206-678-4097. *Innkeepers:* John and Goeff Stone. Open all year.

We always ask innkeepers what their favorite country inn is, and the resounding favorite in the State of Washington is the Captain Whidbey. And with good reason. The Captain Whidbey is the kind of inn one dreams of if one favors the rustic. Here is a fine old turn-of-the-century log structure with more warmth (both visual and human) than you might imagine possible. The building itself is an imposing two-story, twin-roofed beauty constructed of perfectly fitted peeled madroña logs. The madroña, *Arbutus Menziesi*, is a local evergreen tree that bears white flowers and red-orange fruit and was popular with the builder of the inn, Judge Lester Still. He built his inn at the edge of Penn Cove in 1907, and almost immediately the tourists from Seattle began to pour in, borne there by the paddle-wheelers of the day. Tourists continue to pour into the San Juan Islands, today mostly by car.

So great was the Judge's fascination with the madroña that its wood glows richly red in every corner. Not only are the walls and ceilings made of it, but the banisters and the railings as well. Throughout, the wood has been carefully chinked and then given coats of varnish to preserve the sheen. The furnishings throughout the inn reflect the comfort of the turn of the century with handsome period original or reproduction lighting, overstuffed furniture, and antique occasional pieces. The windows have small panes, harmonious with the rustic flavor here. The public rooms include the main living room with broad stone fireplace and early, almost primitive paintings. The Chart Room is an informal bar-lounge with thousands of business cards festooning the walls and ceilings, a dart board, and a crackling fire in the Franklin stove. The dining room has warm wooden tables and a view of the cove below. Dinners served here are from a modest menu that features two daily soups, four standard appetizers, and choice of six entrées that include prime ribs, filet

mignon, ground beef, oysters, poached salmon, and deviled crab. All selections are á la carte, with full dinners (soup, entrée, salad and dessert) ranging from about $8 to $14.

Over the years the inn has added accommodations outside the main building. These include rooms with fireplaces in several cottages and in a recently constructed annex with rooms overlooking the lagoon. All accommodations blend harmoniously into the surroundings. We suspect that many of our readers will prefer the rooms in the main inn for their historic feeling and rustic qualities, but they come at the cost of trips to the hall bathrooms. In all, there are only twenty-four guest rooms here, and reservations are imperative. *Room Rates*: Rooms range from $23 to $50 all year. *Pets*: Permitted in cottages only. *Driving Instructions*: The inn is in Penn Cove, three miles north of Coupville on Whidbey Island. Reach Penn Cove via Route 20 from the north or Route 525 from the south.

Eastsound, Washington

Eastsound is on Orcas Island, in the northern part of the San Juan Island's archipelago. The island is reached by ferry from Anacortes or by air. On Orcas Island is *Moran State Park*, a popular spot for swimming, fishing, and picnicking. *Mount Constitution* has a relatively easy foot trail to its summit at 2,400 feet and is worth the climb for the view of the surrounding islands. The *Orcas Island Historical Museum* in Eastsound presents the history of the island from its Indian period through its settlement by whites in the 1850s. It is open in the summer, and open by appointment only in the other seasons.

OUTLOOK INN
P.O. Box 210, Eastsound, WA 98245. 206-376-2581. Open all year.

This wood-shingled inn, nestling at the edge of the sea on a lovely island, looks as if it had been transplanted from the coast of Maine. The inn has its own private beach, a small pond, and lots of flower gardens at its back side, away from the sea. It was built as the local general store in the mid nineteenth century, and it housed the village jail in the back. There have been several additions over the years.

By 1883 it was operating as a guest house, having dicarded its other functions. In the early innkeeping period, Outlook served as a meeting place for the townspeople. Tradesmen who came to the island by steamer to buy fruit used to rely on the Outlook for home-style cooking and a clean room at the end of the pier. As fruit production waned on the island and tourism gradually took its place, Outlook continued the tradition of providing housing and nourishment to the visitors.

Today the inn continues to offer fine home-cooked meals to guests and the public alike. The hallmark of the food is simple, hearty country fare with large portions and fresh ingredients. There are eleven farm-style breakfasts, featuring fresh eggs, country-smoked bacon, and home-baked breads. Prices at breakfast range up to $4.25 for eggs Benedict but generally fall between $2 and $3. Luncheons offer a selection of sandwiches, but our recommendation would be the soup special. Soups are cooked with care here and seem most appropriate to the seacoast atmosphere. The complete dinner, a real buy, comprises soup or salad, fresh-baked whole grain bread, entrée, and ice cream or sherbet. The entrées include two kinds of fish, steak, a French ragout, German meatballs, pork chops, shrimp, and a selection of omelets. Prices range from $4.75 to $6.95, and at these prices you might consider pulling out all stops and adding apple pie for an additional 90¢.

The eighteen old-fashioned rooms in the inn contain brass or hand-carved beds, marble-top dressers, and collections of period memorabilia. The staff at the inn appreciate plants, which are placed here and there around the rooms to add to the homey feeling. *Room*

Rates: Rooms range from $16 to $24 for double occupancy, all year. *Pets:* Pets are limited; inquire. *Driving Instructions:* Take the ferry from Anacortes to Orcas. Drive north to Eastsound. The inn is in the village.

Index, Washington

Index is a tiny town at the entrance to the enormous wilderness areas of the high *Cascade Mountain Range.* The town is surrounded by towering mountains, beautiful waterfalls, and the white-water *Skykomish River.* It is bordered by the *Upper and Lower Walls,* popular rock-climbers' cliffs of sheer rock rising out of the town. Fishing and white-water rafting are excellent on the river. Index is flanked by *Mount Index* to the south, with its summit at almost 6,000 feet, and *Mount Stickney* to the north—elevation 5,367 feet. The length and breadth of the Cascade Mountain Range are now all national forest and national parkland. Near the town are the breathtaking *Eagle and Sunset Falls.* Hiking, backpacking, and cross-country skiing are good throughout the area. About 30 miles to the east is *Stevens Pass,* at 4,061 feet, from which there is excellent downhill skiing. The road to the ski area, Route 2, goes along the Skykomish River Valley between the mountains on either side.

BUSH HOUSE

5th and Index Avenues, Index, WA. Mailing address: P.O. Box 58, Index, WA 98256. 206-793-0691 and 206-793-9971. *Innkeepers:* Woody and Maurine Sutton. Open all year.

At the base of a sheer mountainside sits the historic old Bush House, built in 1898 by Clarence Bush and his wife to cash in on the big mining and lumber boom in Index. At the turn of the century, Index, then a town of 2,500, was a stopping place along the route of the Great Northern Railroad, traveling through the gigantic Cascade Mountains. The historic Bush House, the post office, and a tavern are all that remain of the boom town, whose population has dwindled to 176.

The hotel stood empty and forlorn for forty years until the Suttons came along. Bush House was then scraped, painted, polished, and scrubbed until it shone. Many of the original hotel furnishings are still here and the Suttons supplemented those with charming European antiques of their own. They have succeeded in recapturing the atmosphere of elegant informality of this fine old hostelry, which has been placed on the state's historic registry.

The restaurant is famous for its home cooking. Maurine Sutton has received so many rave reviews that she's now preparing a cookbook of Bush House recipes. She has incorporated many of the hotel's colorful characters and goings-on into her television script-writing. One favorite of hers is a 400-pound cook who insisted on waltzing about the kitchen singing "Why Not Take All of Me?"

The dining rooms are beautifully decorated with Victorian furnishings of the old hotel along with the Suttons' collection. One room is furnished with Queen Anne furniture right down to the needlepoint cushions of the chairs. A big river-rock fireplace warms one of the rooms, and a wild chandelier created out of 1904 Hupmobile wheels and old wine bottles lights another. There are marble-top tables, thirteenth-century figurines, and a noisy 200-year-old grandfather's clock, which had to be muffled with five layers of felt so that waitresses could hear diners' orders.

Bush House meals are generous and inexpensive. They include a champagne breakfast with a choice of steak and eggs or a variety of omelets all served with hashbrowns, toast, jellies, and hot coffee. Lunches consist of hearty sandwiches and hamburgers. Dinners have a special of the day—perhaps a ham and sweet potato affair or fried chicken. The entrées include steaks, chicken, salmon, and prawns and come with soup or salad, potatoes, home-baked breads, and coffee or tea. Home-baked pies and cakes top off the meal.

Bush House contains ten guest rooms and an eight-bed dormitory complete with all of the original iron beds. The guest rooms are furnished with Victorian antique bedroom furniture. There are old scrolly iron beds and giant high-headboarded oak bedsteads. The dressers came with the hotel, and all rooms share the two old-fashioned hall baths.

The old guest register at the hotel is filled with the names of history's notables who stayed here while on trips through the Cascades. When the lumber companies appeared to be stripping the mountains of all their valuable timber, President Theodore Roosevelt, a dedicated conservationist, traveled to Index to see for himself what could be done to save the mountains from erosion. While there, he stayed at Bush House. It is fun to browse through the register and see who appears there. *Room Rates:* Rooms range from $15 to $40 for rooms that vary from dormitory to enormous double. *Pets:* Only if very well behaved. Be sure to check first. *Driving Instructions:* Index is located about a mile north of Route 2 between the towns of Monroe to the west and Skykomish to the east.

Kalaloch, Washington

Kalaloch is a village in the coastal portion of Olympic National Park. The coastline at this part of the state is particularly rugged and attractive with excellent clamming for razor clams, a local delicacy, as well as exploring tidal pools and beachcombing. Ocean fishing yields smelt during their annual summer runs as well as sea trout and, somewhat later in the season, steelhead. The remainder of the National Park, as well as the surrounding National Forest, is about 30 miles inland, with excellent access from **Quinault**. The inland portion is most noted for its vast rain forests.

KALALOCH LODGE

Route 101, Kalaloch, WA. Mailing address: Star Route 1, Box 1100, Forks, WA 98331. 206-962-2271. *Innkeepers:* Mr. and Mrs. Larry W. Lesley. Open all year.

Kalaloch is the handsomest of the concessioned overnight accommodations within Olympic National Park. The lodge itself is a gray-shingled, two-story building that dates from 1952, when it was built to replace the 1925 original, which had burned. The sprawling lodge sits above an estuary that empties into the Pacific at a point due west of the small village of Forks. While the great bulk of the Olympic National Park is located well inland, there is a narrow strip of park that runs 50 miles south from Ozette. This strip of park provides an immense natural wildlife refuge and contains some of the most beautiful Washington coastline, including a fine beach within a sheltered lagoon that affords excellent swimming.

This portion of the coastline has been visited by the Washington Indian tribes, and the Northwestern Indian theme prevails in the interior of the lodge. The lobby is an inviting, rustic place with stone fireplace. Overnight accommodations range from the eight original rooms in the lodge to a motel unit called Sea Crest House, containing ten modern rooms and suites with private bathrooms and, in the three-room suites, fireplaces. Also available are twenty-eight cabins that vary from semi-modern units with outside toilets to modern fireplace cabins that can house up to nine persons.

The Kalaloch dinner menu draws heavily from the local waters and includes a shore dinner as well as local salmon, king clams, scallops, prawns, Pacific Northwest oysters, and cod filets. In addition there are three steak dinners and spaghetti available for those whose taste does not run to seafood. Entrée prices range from $4.75 to $9.95, with appetizers, soups, and desserts extra.

Kalaloch is an Indian name that may be variously translated as "lots of game," "easy living," or "land of plenty." As you relax in the lodge or private cabin and look out over the ice-blue Pacific stretching endlessly from the bluffs just beyond the lodge, you will probably add your own praises to these left by generations of native Americans. *Room Rates:* Rooms in the lodge range from $26 to $30. The motel-type rooms in Sea Crest are $36 to $42. The better cottages range from $26 to $46. All rates here are for two people. Each additional person brings a charge of $5. *Pets:* Pets are permitted in the cabin area only, and there is a pet fee of $3. *Driving Instructions:* Kalaloch is directly on the coast on Route 101, about 70 miles north of Aberdeen.

Lopez, Washington

Lopez is third largest of the San Juan Islands in Puget Sound. The island is reached by ferry from Anacortes or Sidney, British Columbia. The island offers little to do but enjoy the natural setting and relax from the pressures of society. One pleasant way to do this is to explore the island by bicycle. Rentals are available at Zephyr Cycles. Similarly, one can explore the shorelines in a boat rented at the *Marine Center.* In the summer there is a display of local art at *Grayling Gallery,* and an arts and crafts show is held each August.

BETTY'S PLACE
P.O. Box 86, Lopez, WA 98261. 206-468-2470. *Innkeeper:* Betty Smith. Open all year.

Somehow, with such a prosaic name as Betty's Place, we confess some surprise at the completely international flavor of both the cooking and the guest list at this inn. Recent visitors have included citizens of Iran, most Mediterranean countries, several South American nations, New Zealand, Hong Kong, Canada, and Thailand, to name but a few. When Betty Smith's husband retired from a life that included careers as an executive chef supervising a kitchen staff of forty-three, the wholesale and retail meat businesses, and a grocery business, he and Betty looked around for a place that would allow them to settle and yet remain active. They found a secluded wood-shingled farmhouse on the unspoiled Lopez Island in the middle of Puget Sound and set about to renovate it into a small (two guest rooms) inn. The result is a comfortable home that becomes the home of its guests. The living room is paneled with unobtrusive but modern paneling and has a brick fireplace and a blend of reproduction and antique pieces that span several periods. The two guest rooms are each outfitted with a pair of twin beds.

It is at dinner that one becomes most aware of the chef's talents. The evening meal is his personal choice from a repertoire of more than forty items from a multitude of cuisines. A few of his favorites are beef stroganoff, marinated steaks, baked ham, tenderloin tips with mushrooms, meatballs, oxtails with mushrooms, and selections of creole and gumbo dishes. He often prepares curries from several regions of the world, as well as Mexican, Chinese, and Polynesian dishes. The public is welcome at his table, which can seat up to fourteen, but reservations must be made several days in advance. *Room Rates:* Rooms are $35 for two persons per day, including breakfast and dinner, MAP. *Pets and Children:* Not permitted. *Driving Instructions:* On leaving the ferry landing on Lopez Island, drive along the Island Road for 2 miles to the turnoff for Betty's place.

Mount Rainier National Park (including Paradise, Washington)

Mount Rainier is the majestic centerpiece of Washington, rising 14,400 feet above sea level. Covered with snow and ice the year round, the mountain is one of the best known tourist attractions in the country. This smoldering dormant volcano is still being carved today by storms and by the waterfalls, rivers, and glaciers that sculpt its visage. It is host to fifteen major glaciers, most below the timberline. Elsewhere below the timberline, beautiful meadows of many varieties of wildflowers burst into bloom as the winter snows recede. The height of their colors is reached in late June to early August, when the steep mountain fields glow. In late August the huckleberries, vine maples, and mountain ash turn to the colors of autumn.

In winter only a few roads are kept open—the entrance in Paradise and a road on the northeast near Ohanapecosh. The snows generally begin in November and reach depths of up to 25 feet until the thaw in May. The *Visitors Centers* in Paradise and Longmire are open all year with lectures, exhibits, and films and slides in their auditoriums. At the Nisqually Entrance in the southwest corner of the park, visitors can reach Paradise Valley, where most of the major glaciers are. The Niagra Falls Glacier drops almost 200 feet to the canyon below, carved by the Paradise River. The largest glacier in the continental United States is Emmons Glacier, which can be reached by the Sunrise Road, climbing to almost 7,000 feet.

There are 300 miles of hiking trails here in the park, which offers guided walks and tours in the summer months. Trail guides may be purchased at the centers. Backpackers need permits; the *Wonderland Trail* offers excellent hiking for backpackers and daytrippers on its 91-mile circle around the mountain. The park warns visitors that only experienced mountain climbers should attempt crossing the ice fields and glaciers on a climb to the top. Climbers must register in the park. A snow and ice climbing school run by expert climbers of *Rainier Mountaineering, Inc.*, trains would-be climbers in the summer months. The school furnishes guided summit climbs and five-day climbing seminars. It also rents equipment. For additional information write Rainier Mountaineering, Inc., 201 St. Helens, Tacoma, WA 98402.

PARADISE INN

Mount Rainier National Park, Paradise, WA. Mailing address: 4820 South Washington, Tacoma, WA 98409. Summer: 206-569-2706. Winter: 206-475-6260. *Innkeeper:* Alan W. Schramm. Open from June 15 to Labor Day.

Paradise Inn is a wonder to behold in its mountain setting. The enormous structure was built almost entirely of cedar taken out of one forest. The first section was completed in 1916. Horses were used to drag the huge cedar logs up from the canyon rim to the site. The logs had been salvaged from a forest fire that devastated the area in 1885. The annex was built in 1920, and today the inn provides 117 rooms to guests in the summer months. The lobby and the dining room are of cathedral-like dimensions, fashioned out of Alaskan cedar with huge hand-hewn logs standing in columns supporting the massive beamed ceilings. Most of the woodwork design in the lobby is the work of one man. An old German carpenter, Hans Fraehnke, spent an entire winter in the snow-covered shell of a lodge carving and shaping the cedar logs, using only a hand adze. Two of his outstanding works of craftsmanship stand in the lobby today, a rustic piano and an elaborate grandfather clock. The clock was made in his shop and brought to the inn in three sections. The lobby's beauty is a monument to this Old World craftsman.

The two spacious public rooms offer spectacular views of the mountain and the Tatoosh Mountain Range; the rooms are flanked on either side with rows of high, full-story windows and French doors. The lobby ceiling is completely open and rises to a lofty peak, exposing a crisscross of hand-hewn cedar underpinnings. The room has a second-story mezzanine with comfortable lounge chairs and game tables for cards and checkers on drizzly days and cool evenings. Several large cut-stone fireplaces in the lobby and dining room always have cheery fires blazing in them. The rooms are decorated with painted wooden Alpine designs carved into the massive cedar log supports, and many hand-woven Indian rugs add dashes of bright color to the warm woods.

All but seventeen of the 117 guest rooms have private baths. Mosh of the rooms are newly redecorated and carpeted. The décor and furnishings are modern, complete with ceiling tiles and paneling. There are phones but no television sets. The inn is here for a very special reason, and one look out of a guest-rrom window will show what it is: Spread before you are the sparkling white slopes of Mount Rainier.

A relatively new addition to the inn is the Glacier Room, offering cocktails to both guests and sightseers. The dining room seats two hundred comfortably and serves substantial meals to the many lodgers and tourists who flock here in the warm weather. There are also a souvenir shop and a snack bar. Just a short walk from the inn is the Paradise Visitor Center, a modern, saucer-shaped building. *Room Rates:* Rooms range from $21 to $27, double or single occupancy. Suites of two rooms with shared bath are $37. Each additional person is $5. *Pets:* Not permitted. *Driving Instructions:* In the center of the state, 74 miles from Tacoma and 106 miles from Seattle, the inn can be reached by taking I-5 to Tacoma and then Route 7 south to Route 706 at La Grande. Take Route 706 to Paradise.

Port Townsend, Washington

Port Townsend pokes out into Puget Sound at the tip of the Olympic Peninsula. Today, Port Townsend, a thriving community of 5,800, contains one of the largest collections of Victorian homes in the state. The abundance of fine homes is related primarily to the real estate boom of 1888–89, when the town fancied that it would become the primary shipping port of the West Coast. In fact, for a brief period its shipping tonnage was exceeded only by New York. The population surged to 20,000, but the bottom fell out when the railhead did not locate there. Buildings that had been erected were not occupied above street level, and people left by the thousands.

The town has survived seventy years or more virtually unscathed. Many of the historic old buildings are in private hands and may be viewed only from outside. An interesting exception is the *Rothschild House*, the home of an early wealthy merchant. Built in 1867, the home is open to the public and is maintained by the state. *Fort Worden State Park* comprises of series a Victorian buildings, a school, a theater, and a dirigible hangar. Erected at the turn of the century, the fort was to provide defense for Puget Sound: however, no shots were ever fired here. It is now operated as a conference and recreation center with public fishing, camping, swimming, and picnicking, The *Customs House*, built in 1892, now houses the Post Office. The James House and Manresa Castle are now both operated as inns (see below) and are open to the public for lodging and dining.

JAMES HOUSE

1238 Washington Street, Port Townsend, WA 98368. 206-385-1238. *Innkeepers:* Lowell and Barbara Bogart. Open all year.

The James House is one of the most substantial in Port Townsend, because Francis Wilcox James, who built it in 1889, was a man of substance himself. A self-described "capitalist," he spent $10,000 on his home in a day when most houses cost $2,000 or $3,000. James had been a customs agent, merchant, real estate dealer, and lighthouse keeper. In the latter capacity he had befriended the local Indians who named an island after him.

Lowell and Barbara Bogart took the ferry to Port Townsend from Whidbey Island in August 1976 while on summer vacation. They instantly fell in love with the town, the people, and the setting. After only one night's consideration, they bought the James House. Lowell, a geologist with an oil company, gave up that career with the decision. The family has been innkeeping ever since.

To visit the James House is to step from a busy, loud world into a quiet, gentle place where each of the senses is pleased. Certainly those of sight, touch, and smell are enhanced at every turn here. The inn is a triumph of Victorian splendor. The beautiful woods in the parquet floors and the banisters and wood trim, the elaborately carved period funiture, every mantel piece, each carefully selected wall covering or patterned piece of upholstery—all blend into a visual bouquet. The nose is regaled by the smell of baking bread and by alder burning in the fireplace.

There are a total of ten guest rooms in the house. The prize is the bridal suite, with fireplace, private bathroom, separate sitting room, and a balcony overlooking the bay. On the top floor are four

additional rooms that have breathtaking views of the bay and either the Olympic or Cascade Mountains. The top-floor rooms share two down-the-hall baths with showers. The second floor has, in addition to the bridal suite, two bedrooms that share a bath plus a smaller room with private bath. All the guest rooms have in common a most unusual collection of fine period furniture and one or more of Barbara's house plants. On the lowest floor of the house, formerly an above-ground basement, are a game room and two garden suites. Each suite has two bedrooms, each with two double beds and a bathroom for each suite. One has its own wood-burning stove, and both have views of the water.

If the view from your guest room is not enough, you can sit on the porch and take in Port Townsend Bay, the Straits, Mount Rainier, the Olympics, the Cascades, the Victorian buildings in the historic downtown area, and the ferry traveling back and forth to Whidbey Island. The water is bright blue and the mountains snow-capped. Even in rain the bay has beauty, and the inn seems cozier than ever. Barbara will not let you forget your sense of taste either. You start the day at a large oak table before her beautiful cast-iron wood stove and enjoy a breakfast of one of many homemade breads laden with homemade jelly and served with coffee or tea and orange juice. The gentle sound of the Centurian music box may gently break the silence from time to time, a reminder of Barbara's talent for reawakening the senses to the finer things of life. *Room Rates:* Single rooms are $25, doubles $30, The bridal suite $48, and the garden suites are $38 for two and $48 for four. *Pets and Children:* Children under twelve and pets are not permitted. *Driving Instructions:* Port Townsend may be reached by ferry from Seattle. The ferry disembarks at Winslow. Follow the signs to Port Townsend via Routes 305, 104, and 20. From the Olympic Loop Highway (Route 101) take Route 20 to the center of Port Townsend.

MANRESA CASTLE

7th and Sheridan, Port Townsend, WA. Mailing address: P.O. Box 564, Port Townsend, WA 98368. 206-385-3398. *Innkeepers:* Ronald and Carol Smith. Open all year.

The year is 1892 and Port Townsend is a booming community. Real estate values are soaring, and the lumber business is bringing more and more residents. Charles Eisenbeis has come to town to make his fortune in crackers and brewing, a nicely dovetailed pair of businesses. Nothing will do but the best house in the town for his young bride, and nothing to be found suits the aspiring lord of the manor. So he sets out to build a castle in keeping with his means. Scanning the countryside, he selects the highest point in the area and constructs a turreted castle reminiscent of his native Prussia. The mansion is elegant and possesses a commanding view of the entire town, Puget Sound, and both the Olympic and Cascade mountain ranges. Unluckily for Eisenbeis, the boom period quickly declines, and he is forced to abandon the castle. The castle is sold to the Jesuit order of clergy, who maintain it as a school until the late 1960s, when Ronald and Carol Smith buy the 30,000-square-foot castle and set out to restore the elegance that had long since disappeared. In the process they restore a total of thirty-nine guest rooms and numerous hallways and parlors. To the original structure they fit twenty-seven private bathrooms, so that most of the overnight guests can appreciate the old-fashioned splendor without forgoing modern conveniences.

The castle today is filled with antiques, including scrolly beds, handsome chests, period-style lights, swagged curtains, elaborate carved sideboards, dark wood trim around doors and windows, luxurious carpeting, and copious overstuffed furniture. The effect is opulent, but not offensively so. The opulence is fun, and, after all, it *is* a castle.

The dining room at the inn is set in linen with bentwood chairs and offers a selection of seafood and meat prepared with care. Although some of the seafood is not exotic (salmon, fried oysters, steamed clams), several items are less frequently seen in restaurants outside the region. Certainly most deserving of this designation is the clam steak, a batter-dipped goeduck clam indigenous to the Northwest coast. Among the other pleasant seafood preparations are curried prawns and chicken breasts, Dungeness crab, scallops mornay, crepes Neptune (a blend of scallops, shrimp, crab, and salmon), and cioppino, a San Francisco tomato-based fish stew. From the steak side of the menu comes a choice of five steaks, one served with prawns and a brochette of beef flambé. Complete dinners with appetizer, soup, entrée, and dessert would come to about $15. Service is à la carte, so it is possible to spend more or less, depending on the gluttony of the moment. *Room Rates:* Doubles are $31 to $34, suites

to $46. Additional persons are $6. *Pets:* Small pets are permitted.
Driving Instructions: Take either Route 101 (the Olympic Loop
Highway) or Highway 104 to Route 20; which leads to Port Town-
send. As you enter Port Townsend, the Castle is one block north of
Route 20 on Sheridan Avenue.

PALACE HOTEL

1004 Water Street, Port Townsend, WA 98368. 206-385-0773.
Innkeepers: Liz and Bill Svensson. Open all year.
There have been some wild times at the old Palace Hotel. After a
carefully planned raid on the Palace executed in 1936 by a team of
deputy marshals, the hotel was closed and the owner, one Mary
M——, was unceremoniously ejected from the town following per-
sistent reports of "immoral conditions" at other businesses owned by
the same woman. Times are quieter now, and the Palace has been
restored to a sedate elegance by its current owners. The building is
a three-story Victorian office building constructed in 1889 by Captain
H. L. Tibbals, who was caught up in the building boom of that year.
In fact, he spent the sizable sum of $28,000 building his offices. The
exterior is an example of Richardson Romanesque architectural treatment, and the large arched windows dominate both the exterior and
the rooms inside.

Situated on the waterfront, close to the Keystone ferry, the building is part of the national-historic-site portion of the old business
district. Its first floor is currently occupied by various shops, and
only the two upper floors operate as a hotel. These have been fully
renovated to contain seven guest rooms with Victorian furnishings.
The rooms vary in décor from reproduction wallpapers through exposed brick (a modern treatment but compatible with the period
pieces) to flat-white painted walls. The second floor has a brightly
lighted lobby and a dramatic broad staircase that leads to the third
floor and is lit by an overhead skylight. Four of the guest rooms have
fully equipped kitchens, and four have private bathrooms. Throughout the hotel, the rooms are made even more dramatic by the 14-
foot ceilings, which remind one of the grand level of spending typical
of Captain Tibbals. No meals are served. Liz Svensson is an artist,
and husband Bill is an architect. Their love of clean lines and simple
but tasteful furnishings is evident throughout the hotel. *Room Rates:*
Double-occupancy rates range from $18 to $20 for rooms to $29 for

suites, depending on the time of year. *Driving Instructions:* Follow the instructions listed with the other Port Townsend inns to reach the village. The hotel is in the historic downtown business district.

Quinault, Washington

Quinault is on the fringes of the Olympic National Forest, which borders the Olympic National Park. The surrounding region is part of a vast rain forest. The area receives mors than 12 feet of rain annually (compared to 42 inches in the northeastern United States). The warm, humid-weather and abundance of rain have combined to produce an almost tropical jungle with 300-foot-high douglas firs that tower over a riot of mosses and ferns. Elk are frequently seen in the early morning or late evening. The forest and park provide numerous opportunities for swimming, canoeing, fishing, hiking, and cross-country skiing. *Rivers Northwest,* a local outfitter, provides white-water river rafting on the Quinault and other area rivers.

LAKE QUINAULT LODGE

South Shore Road, Lake Quinault, Quinault, WA. Mailing address: P.O. Box 7, Quinault, WA 98575. 206-288-2571. WATS

reservation number from Washington State only: 800-562-6672.
Innkeepers: Mr. and Mrs. Larry W. Lesley. Open all year.

Although there has been a log hotel on the site since as early as the 1890s to accommodate those coming to Lake Quinault, it was not until 1926 that the main lodge was built. Frank McNeil had visited the Quinault rain forest area on his vacations from the *Seattle Post-Intelligencer,* where he was a linotype operator. He acquired a special permit from the U.S. Forest Service to build and operate a lodge on the current site and then enlisted the financial support of a wealthy lumberman and mill operator named Ralph Emerson. They selected a site that would provide a view of the lake and then began the difficult process of construction. All the materials for the tremendous undertaking had to be hauled over 50 miles of dirt road, and the transportation process was kept up for twenty-four hours a day. A large crew of local and imported craftsmen was hired to put up the hotel, and they accomplished the almost impossible by completing the task in just ten weeks from start to finish.

As one enters the lobby, the great care taken in workmanship is immediately evident from the heavy-beamed wooden ceilings to the bank of small-paned windows that flank the brick fireplace dominating one wall. The room is carpeted, and the large collection of wicker furniture is part of the original collection that McNeil and Emerson installed. Be sure to note the handsome stenciled ceiling. The main lodge is much like a baronial country manor and is the most innlike part of the resort. The forest room is rustic in appearance and contains the main cocktail lounge and bar. The wood-paneled walls are hung with trophies of various hunts, including the heads of elk, moose, and deer as well as an occasional stuffed fish. The dining room has a bank of picture windows giving diners a panoramic view of the lake below. Food in the dining room stresses seafood and includes sautéed prawns, Pacific Northwest oysters, deviled crab, cod filets, and grilled salmon. There are also a selection of the expected grilled steaks and several other nonseafood house specialties such as chicken teriyaki and veal cordon bleu. All meals include the soup of the day, a trip to the salad bar, and an individual loaf of bread. Expect to pay from $6 to $11 (more for the steak or the frozen lobster tail), with appetizers and dessert at additional tariffs. The lodge also has complete à la carte breakfast and luncheon menus.

Overnight accommodations range from the old-fashioned comfort of the twenties-style rooms with their claw-foot tubs to the more modern accommodations in the recently completed annex. All of this was more than good enough for President Franklin Roosevelt when he visited in 1937. He was so inspired that he was moved to create Olympic National Park the following year.

There is much to do amid the "no-need-to-do-anything" atmosphere of the rain forest surroundings. The lodge offers swimming in its large indoor pool; a Jacuzzi whirlpool; men's and women's saunas; a lakefront dock with canoes, rowboats, and paddleboats available; a recreation room with table tennis, pool tables and even a number of modern electronic games; and plenty of trails for hiking. Fishing opportunities are plentiful, with cutthroat, rainbow, and Dolly Varden trout the most frequent prizes. The lake is part of the Quinault Indian Reservation, and a special license must be obtained from the tribe before non-Indians may fish there. A three-day license costs $2.80. The lodge will be happy to arrange one-day float trips down the Quinault River. *Room Rates:* Rooms range from $29 for rooms without bath in the older part of the lodge to $44 in the Fireside Wing for rooms with fireplace. balcony, and private bath. *Pets:* Pets are subject to a size limit and restricted to certain areas. *Driving Instructions:* Quinault is located about 38 miles north of Aberdeen on Route 101. At Quinault, take South Shore Road to the lodge.

San Juan Island (including Friday Harbor and Roche Harbor, Washington)

San Juan island is approximately 15 miles long and 7 miles wide. It is a lovely green gem in the clear waters of the Puget Sound. The island, for its small size, has many acres of parklands and incredibly beautiful scenes at every turn. There are lakes and meadows, miles of breathtaking coastline dotted with natural habors, and pine-covered hills sloping to the crystal-clear waters. The climate is almost always mild here because of warm ocean currents, and some years the temperature never drops below freezing.

Friday Harbor, the county seat, has an active city dock and several marinas for boaters and visitors looking for rentals and charters. Bikes can be rented at the *San Juan Hotel* near the ferry dock. The island has two airstrips, one in Friday Harbor and the other in Roche Harbor; both are within walking distance of the hotels and restaurants.

San Juan Island National Park includes the sites of the American and English camps used during the "Pig Wai," a boundary dispute that lasted twelve years and was finally settled by Kaiser Wilhelm I, who ruled in favor of the United States. The *Friday Harbor Marine Laboratories* are maintained by the University of Washington for research in marine biology. The lab is open to visitors Wednesday through Saturday from 2 to 4 P.M. in the summer. In Roche Harbor, the resort has one of the loveliest harbors anywhere. The marina offers full boating and rental facilities, including a store, laundry, and customs office. The resort provides horseback-riding and hiking opportunities for visitors. Up the hill behind the resort is the unusual *McMillin Mausoleum*. This enormous memorial was built by limestone magnate John S. McMillan and represents his family, his religious credo, and just about everything in which he believed. The resort has a brochure that explains all about the strange chairs around the limestone table and the eerie broken pillar—definitely worth the hike to see it. The island offers visitors unlimited outdoor recreation: excellent skin diving, shell-collecting, fishing, boating, swimming, and driftwood and mushroom gathering. It is a beautiful place to hike or bike around and enjoy the scenery.

HOTEL DE HARO: ROCHE HARBOR RESORT

Roche Harbor, San Juan Island, WA 98250. 206-378-2155. *Innkeeper:* Neil A. Tarte. Open all year.

The Hotel de Haro is a resort hotel that began life as a Hudson's Bay Company trading post. The hotel sits amid beautiful formal flower gardens and overlooks the lovely sheltered harbor and the islands beyond. The original 1845 trading post, forming the heart of the hotel, was expanded in 1886 to a hotel-resort for visiting businessmen in the limestone industry. Limestone was in great demand in the late nineteenth century up and down the coast. John McMillan operated the lucrative limestone empire in Roche Harbor and built the hotel and his own home nearby, which now houses the resort's restaurant. This ivy-covered old hotel has had many distinguished visitors in its day; President Theodore Roosevelt stayed here on various campaign trips to the area.

There is an atmosphere of timelessness here both in the natural setting and in the period décor of the hotel. Three-story verandas wrap around the white-painted wooden building, and ivy twines up and around the railings and pillars. In the foyer is a large fireplace kept burning throughout the cooler months. Antiques befitting the Victorian period are used throughout, and old tapestries and historic photographs of Roche Harbor grace the walls. There are twenty cozy, antique-furnished guest rooms here, four being suites. The suites have private baths and period furnishings, mostly original to the hotel. The Presidential Suite, used by Roosevelt and William Howard Taft, has its own working fireplace and private veranda. Guest rooms have crisp white curtains at the windows, and period wallpapers. They share the old hotel bathrooms down the hall. The furnishings are mostly walnut and oak. There are washstands, marble-top bureaus, enormous old mirrors, and cane-seated rockers and straight chairs. Some of the original love seats are still here also. The front rooms open onto the verandas with views of the harbor.

The restaurant is housed in the old McMillan mansion and is open only in the late spring and summer months. It is a popular dining spot not only for guests but also for the many people whose boats are moored in the harbor (moorings are available for two hundred boats). The restaurant features seafood straight from the beaches and local waters. The specialties are salmon, clams, and prime ribs. The cocktail lounge and restaurant provide stunning views of the harbor activities. There are several snack bars, a cocktail lounge, and a donut shop in the hotel. The big outdoor heated swimming pool and the tennis courts are available to the guests. The marina at the hotel's doorstep offers full boating facilities and rentals. It provides laundry service, showers, and stores for the boating people. Bait and tackle are also available here. The hotel has renovated and attractively furnished several old workers' cottages nearby. They formerly housed limestone quarrymen. The cottages are ideal for families and for longer stays on the island. *Room Rates:* Rates range from $22.50 for the smaller rooms to $43.50 for some suites, EP. Rates are 10 percent less October through April. *Pets:* Not permitted. *Driving Instructions:* There used to be a car ferry to the island, but the service has been discontinued. Private planes can land at the Roche Harbor Airport. Boats dock at the extensive facilities in the harbor.

SAN JUAN HOTEL

50 Spring Street, Friday Harbor, WA. Mailing address: P.O. Box 776, Friday Harbor, WA 98250. 206-378-2070. *Innkeepers:* Norm and Joan Schwinge. Open all year.

The San Juan is a classic old Western hotel. It is conveniently located 100 feet from the ferry landing in Friday Harbor. The hotel, the only one in this harbor town, was built in 1873 and retains the appearance and flavor of the Victorian West. The creaky old wooden building sits beside the street and harbor, clinging to a rather steep hill that slopes to the docks. Although the San Juan gives visitors the feeling of an unspoiled turn-of-the-century establishment, it has been completely restored, renovated, rewired, and replumbed.

The Schwinges are the hotel's newest owners; they purchased the place in December 1978, acquiring an almost totally renovated hotel from the previous owners. There was new wiring throughout, and the bathrooms were brand new with all the modern conveniences unheard of in the hotel's heyday. The building had been repapered throughout with reproduction Victorian wallpaper, and new carpets had been laid.

The Schwinges had ths fun of completely furnishing the place with period furniture to further enhance the antique Western flair of the rooms. Each of the nine guest rooms is individually decorated with Victorian antiques and has its own special character. There are brass beds, old oak and walnut bedsteads, and even old wicker summery headboards. No radio or television intrudes on the peace and quiet of this lovely old harborside rest. The rooms share the two modern hall bathrooms. Views from the curtained windows are excellent. Some of the rooms look out on ths harbor, where the mainland ferry comes and goes. Others have views of the water, steep hills, and the little town. The lobby downstairs has furnishings of the same period and is a nice place to sit and work on a puzzle or read a book. Out in back of the hotel is a private yard where guests can sit and enjoy the sun. The hotel's old well is back here and still pumps water. Guests receive a complimentary breakfast of juice and coffee, which they may enjoy out in the yard if they wish. There are several good restaurants in town and on the rest of the island. The local specialty is, of course, the fresh seafood of the island. Many restaurants and shops are within walking distance of the hotel. The ferry and airport are also nearby, so visitors can comfortably come without a car. The hotel rents out bicycles for touring the island, and the marina offers all manner of boating facilities. Guests can fish right off the dock by the hotel. *Room Rates:* The Schwinges were not sure of the rates at the time of publication but said they would be in the range of $24 for a double with continental breakfast. *Pets:* Only the best behaved housebroken pets are allowed. *Driving Instructions:* Ferries leave Anacortes every few hours for the one hour and fifty minute cruise through the San Juan Islands to Friday Harbor. There is also a ferry from Sidney, British Columbia, to Friday Harbor. The airport is 3/4 mile from town. Friday Harbor provides complete docking facilities for private boats.

Stehekin, Washington

Stehekin is the northernmost outpost on Lake Chelan and the gateway to the North Cascades National Park. Lake Chelan is a 55-mile expanse of azure blue, filling a gorge that averages less than 2 miles wide but dips to more than 1,500 feet in places. The lake is fed by twenty-seven glaciers and fifty-nine streams and is one of the most scenic in the Northwest. In addition, it is bordered on both sides by National Forest land and has thereby been spared the scarring effects of development.

The Stehekin Valley was first explored in 1814 by the British fur trader Alexander Ross. The valley is under the supervision of the National Park Service, which operates a 22-mile shuttle bus service up the valley. The *National Park Visitor Center* offers interpretive talks and displays, horseback riding, and horse pack trips. There are local craft shops, and guided tours of the *Buckner Homestead* and the local one-room schoolhouse, the only one still used in the State of Washington, are available. At the schoolhouse, the only one still used in the State of Washington, are available. At the opposite end of the lake (reached by passenger ferry) is the village of Chelan. The main business of the Chelan area is the harvesting of approximately 10,000 acres of orchards planted, largely, with red and golden delicious apples.

The only way to reach the Stehekin Valley is by the ferry or plane service described in the discussion of the lodge that follows.

NORTH CASCADES LODGE

Box 275, Stehekin, WA 98852. 509-662-3822. *Innkeepers:* The Gibsons and the Dinwiddies. Open all year.

North Cascades Lodge is a rustic Nationl Park Lodge near the northern tip of Lake Chelan in North Cascades National Park. Getting here is half the fun. There are no roads to the lodge, and the guest's arrival depends on either a four-hour ferry ride on the *Lady of the Lake* (509-682-2224), which departs from the village of Chelan 50 miles to the south or by seaplane from the same village. A pleasant compromise between speed and the more leisurely boat trip is to fly up from Chelan on *Chelan Airways* (509-682-5555) and return by boat, well rested from your stay at the remote lodge. Ferry service to Stehekin is daily in the summer and Monday, Wednesday, Friday, and Sunday from October 15 to May 15.

North Cascades Lodge is one of the last resorts to be reached only by boat or plane. It is a rambling collection of rustic, wood-faced one-and two-story lodge buildings plus some detached housekeeping cabins. The setting is spectacular. There are many places in America that inspire visitors to call them "little Switzerland." This certainly is a contender for the title. This is the land of the Cascade red fox, spry mountain goats, bobcats, eagles, osprey, ruffed grouse, and great gray owls. Once ensconced in your comfortable, wood-paneled lodge room you are free to do absolutely nothing. Listen, as they say, to the stillness of Stehekin. Then you may enjoy the beauty of the surrounding park. There are practically unlimited hiking, boating, and fishing. The mountains are broken by the Stehekin Valley at this point, and a bus tour is available through the surrounding dirt roads during warmer weather with stops along the Stehekin River and at Rainbow Falls. Be sure to take your camera. The lodge will be happy to arrange river rafting and horseback pack trips in the warmer months.

In the winter, the lodge remains open with the emphasis on winter ski touring. The lodge offers basic instruction with certified instructors as well as weekend and midweek holiday ski-lodge packages. For experienced skiers, the lodge offers the Courtney Ski Trip, which includes two nights at the lodge and two nights in a rustic cabin with guided tours and meals provided.

The lodge dining room offers a modest American-style menu with the emphasis on hearty home cooking. Featured are chef's salad, shrimp or crab Louis, miner's stew (a lodge specialty), fried chicken, baked ham, shrimp, and steak. From the simple dessert menu, the Washington nut pie, a lodge tradition, is perhaps the best bet. *Room rates:* Single rooms are $24, Double rooms $30, and suites $42. Housekeeping units are $3 more than the above rates. Additional people are $6 except children under eleven, who are $3 additional. *Pets:* Not permitted. *Driving Instructions:* No automobile access. (See above.)

Index of Inns

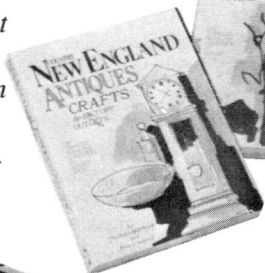